Robert Time

The Tree Farm

Little, Brown and Company

Boston · Toronto

THE TREE FARM

Robert Treuer

Drawings by
Sandra Sandholm Reischel

FIRST EDITION

T05/77

The author is grateful to Little, Brown and Company for
permission to reprint "Song of the Open Road" from *Verses
from 1929 On* by Ogden Nash. Copyright 1932 by Ogden Nash.

"Tree Farm" is a registered service mark of the American
Forest Institute.

Library of Congress Cataloging in Publication Data

Treuer, Robert.
    The tree farm.

    Autobiographical.
    1. Treuer, Robert. 2. Tree farms—Minnesota.
3. Minnesota—Biography. 4. Country life—
Minnesota. I. Title.
SD129.T74A35   977.6'78 [B]   76-52959
ISBN 0-316-85273-2

Designed by D. Christine Benders

*Published simultaneously in Canada
by Little, Brown & Company (Canada) Limited*

Dedicated to my family,
especially my parents, Fritz and Mia,
and to those who died in the concentration
camps 1939-1945.

Contents

Preface

The Tree Farm is a true account of events and relationships since the farm's beginning in 1958. Some incidents are telescoped to make the essentials more comprehensible; personalities have been combined and names changed to protect the privacy of friends and neighbors.

The account is topical and not always chronological because the passage of time is only of personal interest except as it bears on events. Some chapters therefore do not appear in time sequence: "Work Bee" happened in the second year, "Dog Pack" in the third, and "Fire" also took place early on. This may explain why our younger sons, Tony and David, do not appear in some of the chapters (they had not yet been born), and why our older sons, Smith, Paul, and Derek, are visitors in other incidents (they had by then grown and established lives elsewhere).

Some of the happenings in *The Tree Farm* occurred during the years of my first marriage, to Nancy; others during my present marriage, to Peggy. I used Peggy's name where appropriate and other times the literary device "my wife," referring sometimes to Peggy, more often to Nancy. Nancy shared the tree farm endeavors and this life during her years here. I appreciated it then and do so now. Many people have given to and received from the tree farm. I think we're all the richer for it.

Readers interested in the more technical aspects of tree farming are referred above all to their local county extension office. Extension staff are sensitive to local geography, climate, soil, and economy. Some offices have foresters on the staff, and all have working relationships with state forestry and conservation organizations and with the United States Department of Agriculture, with its experts, research facilities, and support programs. The extension staff will also know what state university or college resources are available, and what nurseries, timber, and paper companies have to offer. Among private organizations, the American Forest Institute (1619 Massachusetts Avenue NW, Washington, D.C. 20036) and the American Forestry Association (1319 Eighteenth Street NW, Washington, D.C. 20036) will be helpful.

My thanks to foresters and conservationists William Sliney, Maurice Blackburn, and Bob Wennerstrand for instructing and helping me as a tree farmer; to the U.S. Agricultural Extension Service and its staff in

Bemidji; and to the Minnesota Department of Natural Resources and its good and dedicated people.

My respected friend Farrell Creech, retired from a lifetime career with the U.S. Forest Service at the Chippewa National Forest, read this manuscript and succeeded in pointing out to me some of my errors. His willingness to share his knowledge has been a sweetener of my life; and the balance between nature, intellect, and people that he and his wife Dr. Lila Gorenflo Creech have achieved has been an example for me and others to follow.

Dr. Sherman Paul, University of Iowa teacher, critic, and author, encouraged and instructed me in the writing of this book. The Little, Brown editor of *The Tree Farm* is William D. Phillips, whose work and patience have helped to bring smoothness and consistency to the manuscript, and whose counsel and friendship have been invaluable.

The Tree Farm seeks to convey what it feels like to establish such an enterprise and to fashion such a way of life — how it affects us and others; the book also deals with ecological and aesthetic values, so that you may do your own reflecting and reach your own conclusions, illuminated and entertained in some measure by our experiences.

The Tree Farm

1

Signpost

It is 200 acres of northern Minnesota sandhills on the Mississippi River at a place where you can still walk across the stream. Near our north fence line is the spot where the river first turns south after flowing north and east on a winding course of a hundred miles from its source at Lake Itasca. When you drive past the tree farm on a sandy country road it is not spectacular and melds into the rest of the countryside of pine forests, lakes, and occasional farm fields. There is a small lake of about five acres which is deep and spring-fed and which nestles in a pine plantation. You pass it in seconds. During the brief summer many people come to vacation in this area. Then in late fall, usually around Thanksgiving, the lakes freeze over until the thaw at the end of April. This is my home.

It's finally been certified as an official tree farm, and my young sons Tony and David are helping me set a post at the driveway entrance and nail up the green and white diamond-shaped sign pronouncing this day what has been fact for over sixteen years. My wife, Peggy, takes a picture.

"It's like a marriage ceremony after you've had several children," I say, but Peggy doesn't think this appropriate in front of the children. I try for other analogies but they are worse and she goes back to her interrupted legal work.

Usually certification of a tree farm takes place at the beginning, but we had never bothered to see to it or to post a sign. It seemed unimportant then and seems only moderately important now — a flying of the flag for conservation, and a notice to Christmas tree seekers and other marauders that these trees aren't here by accident. Better late than never, and official certification doesn't change what we will do here, or what we have done here, or what happened before we arrived.

Long ago the glaciers of the last ice age blanketed this land in all directions, making an arctic of what was to become north woods. As the glaciers began to thaw, runoff water was blocked from its northward egress, and it collected in a huge, temporary lake named Agassiz, after the Swiss geologist who in the last century discovered the still-recognizable lakeshore; the lake itself disappeared when enough glacier ice had melted to allow the water to drain into Hudson Bay. The easternmost boundary of Lake Agassiz is nearly fifty miles west of us, and it is fertile plain and fairly flat.

North of us nearly a hundred miles is the Canadian border, and there the Precambrian granite tilts close to the earth's surface. There the dying glacier, grinding and gouging in its protracted throes, carved deep and spectacular lakes shored by granite cliffs.

South of us there are gentle hills and sand country drifting down to the twin cities of Minneapolis and Saint Paul over two hundred fifty miles away. Here at the tree farm and all around us the countless lakes are also presents of the last ice age, as are the sand and gravel — the moraines dumped and squeezed by the ice age blanket.

The melting of the glaciers left only one massive lake for a while, and when the land reemerged there were undulating hills among the streams and lakes where gradually, over ten thousand years or so, the north woods came to be. Then at the turn of this century the forests were cut, converted to marginal farms plagued by thin soil and intemperate climate. Now the forests are returning, as farms falter and fail.

A half mile away from our east fence line is the boundary of Leech Lake Indian Reservation, where Peggy was born and raised, and where her sizeable family lives.

Peggy's mother arrives unannounced at dinnertime, her car loaded with groceries, sleeping bags, and camping gear. It's one of the pleasures of having lots of family around. They drop in, we drop in. When we leave the house the door is left open and a kitchen-table note pad announces where we have gone and when we expect to return. Visitors then use their discretion on whether to wait or leave a note. We've often come home from outings to find the house full and dinner on the stove ready for us.

"It's too crowded and noisy back in town," Peggy's mother announces. (Town is the village of Bena with a population of 186.) "It's so nice and quiet here."

I know from past experience that the tent won't be put up and that the gear will stay in the car while she sleeps in the house. As a matter of fact, I can't recall a time when Peggy's mother, Luella, has actually slept in that tent. But she brings it along and I think it gives her a feeling of going camping.

"I see you've got a tree farm sign up," she remarks. "I suppose you'll be going to the barn to milk the trees."

That's mild compared to the good-natured teasing I'll be getting from Peg's rough-and-tumble cousins, so I'd better brace myself.

Tony and David swarm over their grandmother and help unload groceries while I enjoy the spectacle. Luella looks like a full-blooded Chippewa; her coloring, black hair, and features are classic and while she isn't tall, her thin, rangy build gives the illusion of height. By contrast, Peggy's hair is dark brown, tinting auburn in summer, and her skin is paler, but she shares with her mother the illusion of height. Tony has his grandmother's coloring, bone structure, and complexion, while David has bright red hair, pale skin, and my stocky build.

After dinner Luella and I play Scrabble in our endless contest; we each collect and hoard words during

days between games. The children are playing quietly
and Peggy is poring over law books and legal briefs.
She is the only Indian person from her village to have
gone beyond high school and on to a successful profes-
sional career, first as a registered nurse, then as health
program administrator, and now as an attorney specializing in Indian law.

"Pretty rugged camping," I comment to Luella. "It's
so cold and looks like it'll storm, and there're bears and
wolves . . ."

"It's your turn to play, and you can give me thirty-
nine points," she says, turning the Scrabble board on
the lazy Susan, which is used only for that purpose.

The tree farm sign is giving rise to more jibing than
I'd anticipated. W.H. Nelson, fellow teacher from the
days when I taught at Cass Lake High School, and
two artist friends from Minneapolis, Marlon Davidson
and Don Knutson, are over to play bridge. They propose I replace the offending sign with a hired spider,
a la *Charlotte's Web*, to spin TREEMENDOUS; and they
regale me chorus fashion with a rendition of Ogden
Nash's doggerel:

> *I think that I shall never see*
> *A billboard lovely as a tree,*
> *For unless someday billboards fall*
> *I'll never see a tree at all.*

W.H. towers over me by a foot, his hair crew cut
and gray where mine is long and black. Students used

to refer to us as "Mutt and Jeff," but never to our faces.

I take the banter as intended. They have been my friends for many years and remember the struggles and hard times I've had along with the good. We've walked together among the trees that are now twenty- and thirty-foot-tall Norway pine — among trees standing in fields where we have walked together before, when the fields were empty and we could see across them half a mile to the farmstead. They'd witnessed some of the early plantings: 25,000 in 1959 when the fields had stood empty save of weeds and grass, that many again the next year and the two after that. Then came disastrous 1963, when the nursery had an oversupply and all of us on long-term planting programs were urged to accelerate. I was scheduled for 65,000 trees. We worked hard, in bad weather, but that summer's drought killed all the seedlings and in 1964 we had to do it all over, the planting machine bumping over the previous year's furrows with the dead tufts reminding us of the loss.

"If you have a poor hand, just pass," W.H. interrupts my reverie in his customary sardonic manner.

"Or are you worried some of your trees have strayed into the neighbor's pasture?" Marlon asks. Marlon's geniality masks a successful artist, a man of discipline and talent, just as W.H. uses his sarcasm and acid wit as camouflage — he is a brilliant intellectual, teacher, and art connoisseur. Our isolated northern community has attracted a wide spectrum, a galaxy of humankind. Our interests, vocations, and avocations range from the outdoors to the most esoteric of intellectual and artistic pursuits; our backgrounds and cultural origins range as widely, and among the riches we share are elements of companionship, respect, and regard for privacy.

Marlon and Don ask about the recent harvest of pulpwood in the northwest corner, which left ugly scars and piles of slashings — the residue of unused branches and treetops.

"It was a scrubby stand of trees, a mix of jack pine and aspen coming up at random after a long-ago cutting, long before I came here," I explain. "The trees would never amount to much, and we'll put in a planting of Norway pine next spring. About ten thousand." Profits from the sale will pay for the seedlings, and the paper companies provide an unending market for the pulpwood.

Once land is cut or burned over, a dominance (or succession) cycle starts from ground zero, with grasses giving way to shrubs, which in turn give way to leafy softwood trees and jack pine; ultimately taller species shade and crowd the predecessors until the species dominant in that particular soil and climate asserts itself. It's an endless competition for sunlight and soil nutrients, and therefore for space. Among trees, as with humans, there come times when the king must die.

The process in its natural form takes hundreds of years, but nature's timetable can be foreshortened by a forester or tree farmer who plants the most productive later-sequence trees that will flourish. There are many ways of doing this, depending on how rich the soil is, on how hospitable the growing season is, and most of all on what is on the land in the first place. If the land is open field or pasture, it is only a question of deciding what species to choose, and then proceeding to plant by machine or by hand.

If there already are trees on the land, they can be selectively cut and the open spots underplanted or spot-planted. *Underplanting* consists of hand-planting seedlings of a more aggressive, dominant species under the umbrella of existing and less desirable trees; the existing trees will over the years be crowded out and eventually supplanted by the newcomers. *Spot-planting* usually refers to the hand-planting of seedlings in open patches, or in places where an uneven "take" in a plantation has left gaps.

Clear-cutting (removing all the trees standing) and then replanting is a dangerous practice, because it devastatingly disrupts wildlife and flora, opening the door to traumatic erosion by removing the natural rain catchers and absorbers provided by trees, and because the heavy tree-removal equipment compacts the soil so as to make new growth more difficult. However, clear-cutting is sometimes necessary, because there are some species of trees so shade-intolerant that they cannot establish themselves as part of a man-made foreshortening of the dominance cycle unless there is no competition for sunlight. This makes the issue of clear-cutting quite complicated at times from a pragmatic viewpoint — not to mention the ethical considerations involved in weighing the advantages to wood users against the ecological disadvantages.

Other planting techniques are: to spray existing
shrubs and trees with herbicide and then to underplant, or to first underplant and then suppress or control the existing species by hand-cutting, pruning, or
spraying. I've become increasingly convinced over the
years that herbicides are dangerous to wildlife and
man, and I have concluded that they are dangerous as
well to the very trees I am seeking to establish. (My
conclusion may be questionable, but I cherish my
opinions with enthusiasm even when their factual base
may be open to debate.)

For us, the most productive late-sequence species to

establish is the Norway (or red) pine, the soil being too light and sandy to sustain spruce except in scattered spots. White pine would be the ideal tree — even better than Norway in the quality of the wood and in its natural growth capability in this climate and soil — except that it is highly susceptible to widespread blister rust. But the Norway pine is not a bad tree at all: straight-trunked, long-needled — a noble and handsome tree.

"At Lake Itasca they've been protecting the trees in the park," I explain to city dwellers Marlon and Don. (Itasca is thirty-five miles southwest of us by road, but over a hundred miles by canoe as the little river meanders.) "Now the groves of huge Norway pine are being endangered by birch, which come later in the dominance cycle."

"That'll teach you to ask him a question," Peggy offers. "You get a lecture."

"And I'm still waiting for him to bid this hand," says W.H., scuffing his feet on the carpet in impatience, "before daybreak. Or perhaps before the next species in the dominance cycle of trees makes its appearance."

I must make an effort to cultivate more respectful friends. To think I have to put up with this chaffing just because I posted a tree farm sign at my driveway entrance . . .

2

Seedbeds

I T HAD NOT STARTED out as a tree farm at all, nor as my home.

In the summer of 1957 I began scouring the area around Bemidji and Cass Lake, Minnesota, for tax-forfeited land. I had canoed in the boundary waters for years, the trips getting longer and more venturesome, and many of my other interests had to do with the outdoors: a modest amount of skiing, hiking, mountain climbing, and camping.

The Bemidji area was close enough to canoe country to put it easily within a day's drive, and the gentle hills and many lakes, the remnants of great forests and promise of future ones, appealed to me. And so did the challenge of winter and wilderness. I had come to love the area, but I could only afford to buy some land if it were inexpensive.

Bemidji and Cass Lake originated as logging towns shortly before the start of this century, sited on ancient

Indian camping grounds. Bemidji ultimately grew into a commercial and educational center for north-central Minnesota, with a population hovering around ten thousand excepting summer tourists and visitors. Cass Lake, a significant railroad town during the heyday of logging, shrank again with the disappearance of the big timber and is a village today, hosting the headquarters of the Chippewa National Forest. The two communities are fourteen miles apart, interspersed by lakes, rivers, woods, some resorts, and a few farms.

My search for tax-forfeited property did not produce any hopeful results. There were parcels of swamp and cutover land; some were difficult to locate, and none came anywhere near the idyll of my dreams, though I was hard put to explain just what this utopia had to look like.

The patient staff in the county courthouse at Bemidji finally ran out of property listed as tax-forfeited, and gently asked me if I had talked to the Farmers Home Administration — they might know of farms that had failed.

A kind but skeptical FHA official took his time with me. "Are you interested in farming?" Farms were failing throughout the area then; many farmers were unable to keep up with mortgages and a few were forfeiting on FHA loans. I realized that he was concerned that here might be yet another loan applicant, and one who knew nothing about farming.

"No, I'm just interested in some land where we could come in the summer," I told him. "Either to camp or to put up a cabin. I'm interested in the out-

doors and conservation, and I would like to have a place
of my own."

He seemed relieved. "I know of two places between
here and Cass Lake. Both are deserted farms." My
heart leaped at the mention; I had been asking around
for such places. He detected my excitement and went
on:

"The one is the Wold farm, about one hundred sixty
acres. It's been empty for quite a while, and if you are
interested after you've seen it, I'll help you get in
touch with the owners. The other one is about a mile
away and is in pretty bad shape. It's two hundred
acres, and we will be selling it in a sealed-bid auction
in a few months; the owners forfeited on the mortgage.
Everything was auctioned off except the land, and
that'll be going next."

"What's so bad about it?"

"Well, why don't you take a look, and then we can
talk."

A ten-mile drive, the last few miles down washboard-
like, dusty sand roads, took me to the Wold farm.
It was flat land, and a large, two-story clapboard house
was situated an eighth of a mile back from the road,
surrounded by large white pines. Behind the empty
and vandalized house were tumbledown barns and
outbuildings, and a shallow pond. This was the kind of
place I had been looking for — yet why didn't I respond to it, react in some way? I walked around and
mulled the possibilities, envisioning the appearance
with the outbuildings removed, the house fixed up, a
canoe on the pond, which was three or four acres in

size. But then I turned away, disappointed once again, and headed back to town.

A crossroad sign jogged my memory, and looking at my notes, I found that this road would lead me to the other deserted farm, the one that was in such bad shape. What had he said it was called? The Stough farm. The short drive brought me through fallow, weedy fields on rolling terrain, with outcroppings of brush and woods here and there, to a lovely little lake set deep among the hills, and clearly visible from the road. I stopped to admire the setting, especially the tall trees on the hillsides opposite. There was a drive-way lined by shading Norway pines on my left, and on a whim I turned in, realizing only then that this was the Stough farm I had been trying to locate.

At the end of the driveway there was a grotesque, tumbledown wood structure that I soon discovered had been a machine shed and garage. It was filled with broken machinery and discarded parts, and stank of rot, mildew, and bats. The driveway turned right into the farmyard, which was waist-high in weeds. The hip-roofed barn was sagging, leaning sadly, and sway-backed. The house was wooden, its siding curled, and once upon a time long ago its windows and doors had disappeared. A smaller house on a high cement basement seemed sturdier, but it was unfinished inside and filled to windowsill level with open fertilizer bags, broken machinery, and furniture thrown in helter-skelter. Other outbuildings in even greater disrepair dotted the farmyard.

Wherever I stepped there were rusted tin cans, heaps of ashes and partially burned trash, and the stench of refuse — the sickly sweet smell of a garbage dump. But when I raised my eyes from all this there were the stately pines lining the driveway and else-where about the yard a few large spruce which had been spared when the yard was cleared. And beyond this the rolling hills — dipping to little marshes and creeks, and across the road to the lake. I set out to walk these hills and fields, and found natural groves of trees, containing mainly Norway pine and spruce over a hundred years old and also some very old white pine and tamarack. Behind one of these groves was a second lake, twin to the first; there was a clear water creek bubbling between the two lakes, then flowing out of the second one to . . . where? I made my way through the brush and marsh and emerged on the Mississippi, seventy or eighty feet across, with a shallow island in the middle and a bend where the creek came out. The opposite shore was woods, marsh — and un-developed.

"I want the Stough farm," I told the FHA official.

"The buildings are totally useless," he said. "We have put no value at all on them."

I nodded my head, trying to keep from smiling with excitement and happiness.

"You also should know that the land is very poor. Of the two hundred acres only seventy or eighty are high enough to be cultivated —"

"That's fine!"

". . . and they won't produce much. The rest is low-land and brush; there are only a few good trees left. The former owners had hoped to pasture cattle in the marsh — marsh grass can be good feed. But it floods out every spring, and in a wet year is useless all year."

I kept grinning insipidly and nodding my head.

"The place is infested with noxious weeds that have to be eliminated. All told, I do not consider it to have any potential as an income-producing farm," he con-cluded.

"I want it!"

"Well, it'll be coming up for sale soon. I'll send you the papers and if you want to submit a bid, just follow the directions that I will enclose. But remember what I've told you."

"I will," I assured him. "I want it."

He looked at me dourly, skeptically, and remarked that "others have been interested too. But if you don't change your mind the way they did, you may be the only one."

I was. It was the end of winter and the coming of spring before the paper process had run its course; mine had been the only bid and I had offered — not knowing what relative land values were — all that I felt I could afford, hoping that this would suffice. It came to a little over $2,000 and the amount had to be increased in order for the offer to be considered. But ultimately the farm was mine, and I had in my possession the tattered abstracts of title tracing all the prior ownerships (except the original Indian one), and recording on the last page my own — temporal though human proprietorship and possession may be.

The transaction was signed, sealed, and delivered one day after much fretting and worrying (for which I have a proclivity). I breezed into my office in Sheboygan, Wisconsin (where I was working for the United Auto Workers as a union representative), with the same frozen grin paralyzing my face as had that day many months before when I had returned to the Bemidji FHA office after my first visit to *the* farm. My closest friend and work associate, Leo Breirather, chief steward of the union local on strike at the Kohler Company, took one look at me and said: "Congratulations! I see you got it. Now you'll always have a place of your own — a place you can call home!"

Is that what I had done? Gotten a place that would be the one where I could set roots, where I would always be at home? I thought I'd gotten a summer place, a spot I could go to and camp, where I could indulge my love of the outdoors. Was my unspoken need for a place of my own, for a sense of permanence, so obvious? Leo knew me well through four years of close association and always spoke with thought and care. His remark caused me pause, and set me to a deeper reflection on the significance of *the* farm. I was a young man well along on a successful career that satisfied my yearnings to change the world and make it better. Why would my closest friend seem to think I was somehow unfulfilled and looking for something else? It was a question I had better ask of myself, where the answers lay.

About then the union decided to terminate the picketing. I was ordered to transfer to Detroit, the strikers were to return to work at the factory after five years of picketing, and the issues in the conflict that had not been resolved during years of economic, political, and public-relations combat would be presented to the National Labor Relations Board and the American judicial process for resolution. Detroit? Who wanted to live in Detroit? In Sheboygan I was at least close to the Horicon Marsh and the small mountains near Devil's Lake, and only a day's travel from northern Minnesota's canoe country. But Detroit? That meant a huge city, working in a big office under close supervision and becoming even further enmeshed in the organizational discipline inherent in all institutions. What did I really want of life? What kind of person had I become? What had I told Leo anyhow?

I was born in Vienna, Austria, an only child. My mother was a successful music teacher and educator; my father was a shopkeeper active in liberal politics, whose many friends gathered in his store and looked up to him as a well-read, idealistic, and gentle man. Unfortunately, they did not purchase much from his store. The fascist coup of the middle thirties clouded and circumscribed our lives and, though I did not know it at the time, brought my father into active work in the underground. When the Nazis took over in 1938 we were endangered not only because we were Jews, but also because my father's politics were well known. My mother and I escaped to England, where I narrowly evaded deportation and concentration camp because the Jewish school which was to harbor me did not know what to do with a child who had no religious training. My father disappeared into the Austrian countryside under an assumed identity as a farm laborer, and ultimately escaped and joined us. He would never speak of what he had witnessed and experienced.

We came to the United States just before World War II erupted, settling in Yellow Springs, Ohio, after a short stay in New York, and my parents established their new lives through very hard, sometimes menial, work. Though their jobs changed, a constant factor in our lives was the big garden with grafted fruit trees, for my father had a green thumb and a love of growing things, which stemmed from his intellectual rapport with Nature and from his peasant, countryside forebears. This love he sought to impart to me from my earliest childhood on. We also raised bees, kept chickens, canned, and took it for granted that this was necessary and that long hours were the natural way of life. Though I was a high school student then, I worked after school and during the summers. My father ultimately obtained a job as a shipping clerk, which he held for twenty-five years without missing a day's work, while my mother rose to become a widely known business executive and a pioneer in the use of computers.

When the war was over we attempted to locate the remainder of our family through the Red Cross and various refugee organizations. Of my generation, three cousins had survived, though I was the only Treuer. Of my parents' generation, two of my uncles and two aunts had escaped. My father's father, a tenacious old man, had remained in Vienna and had outlived the Nazis — hiding toward the end in a coal bin, only to die shortly after surviving the ordeal. The rest of our extended and extensive family had been killed in the concentration camps; we collected the information in sporadic telegrams and messages from Red Cross searches during the following months.

The course of my adolescent life lacked the straight-line direction of my parents' lives. I floundered, groped, rebelled, and lashed out, leaving home the first time at sixteen, dropping out of high school to enter college, becoming involved in radical and militant activities wherever they found me or I found them. By eighteen I was married, was a father, and was serving in the army, dreaming of heroism but not really distinguishing myself; by twenty-one I had three children, and had completed my college residency requirements but had no degree; however, I had enough idealism and self-righteousness to carry me where the facts of a given situation would not.

I became editor of the *Wisconsin CIO News* and oversaw its growth to a weekly circulation of nearly thirty thousand. I used its space to espouse my beliefs about racial justice, reapportionment, tenants' rights, and redress wherever I perceived injustice and exploitation. When the United Auto Workers organized and later struck the Kohler plumbing-fixtures firm near Sheboygan, I wasted no time in putting in my two cents' worth. It was a large company, owned at that time by one man; located in a company-dominated village a few miles from Sheboygan, its high, prisonlike walls were excrescent on the farming countryside. This could have been the Europe of my childhood, the ancient enemy all over again: exploited and oppressed laborers at the mercy of the feudal baron, the specter of anti-Semitism, superstition, and hatred. The UAW offered me a job and I sold my home in Milwaukee, moved to Sheboygan, and became more ardent in the cause of the strikers than the most put-upon worker in the plant.

Then came the day for the strike as such to end and for me to become a more disciplined member of the organization that employed me — an organization which I had fought and resisted at times as much as I did the management of the struck firm. And this happened when I was seriously questioning myself about what I was doing with my life, and why, and how; and when a touch, a whiff of Walden seemed within my reach. It was a time when I felt my three sons growing farther away from me, when I felt myself only minimally involved in their growing up; and a time when I felt my marriage deteriorating further — for it had been difficult at times. We had discussed divorce, which my wife at times thought might be the wiser course, but which was an admission of failure I could not accept. But one image from that time haunted me above all.

There had come a moment during the strike, some three years before, at the height of conflict and passion, when a demonstration I had helped to plan and stage erupted unpredictably into a rampaging riot I could not control or stop. It ran its course through the day and the night until it ebbed and ended. In the small hours of the night I walked the littered and deserted streets, persuading the last of the stragglers to go home, and was about to do so myself, when a solitary figure came ambling by, shuffling down the darkened streets where all lights had been broken during the day. He wove his way among the wrecked cars and trucks, sidestepping the debris, mewling and moaning in his inarticulateness — a victim of both severe retardation and an untreated harelip. He was a familiar figure in the town, and here he was now, reacting to the excitement and confusion with his animalistic response, unwittingly and uncognitively wailing, seeking to utter the unutterable. He approached me and kept coming — our eyes did not lock as he passed — and I heard him fade into the distance, his inchoate sounds absorbed by the night.

For nigh unto three years the image of the idiot plagued and troubled me, and made me ask of myself how much of my life was really given to being *constructive* in my work, my beliefs, and my personal relations — and how much was a knee-jerk reaction, an automatically repeated fight against things that were bad simply because they symbolized the enemies of my childhood. Was my own reaction to life and society like that of the mewling retardate? Cost what it might, I had to resolve my self-doubts, my questions to myself about my goodness and my worth.

I decided to move up north and carve out, somehow, a new life for myself: a life that would enhance closeness for all of us in the family, that would give me in its daily living an intimacy with the elements and the land, in which I could find more constructive ways of exercising my beliefs about social justice and individual human dignity. The three boys agreed enthusiastically, though warned about the hard work ahead, much as the FHA official had warned me about the farm. My wife would have preferred doing this someplace in the Caribbean rather than in northern Minnesota — a suggestion that sent my immigrant and refugee anxieties to the ceiling, for in those days I dreaded even crossing into Canada for an outing, in fear that I would not be readmitted to the United States. In the end we all agreed we would move to the farm, somehow fix a house out of all the buildings there, and somehow earn a living.

"What'll you do?" friends had asked as they saw us off in Sheboygan.

"I'll write a book!"

"Tell 'em all about Kohler!"

"Sure, I'll do that."

"I wish I could come up and help you a few days," Leo said. He had a more realistic assessment than I did of what I was up against in my decision to some-how remodel the condemned buildings, of which I had shown him pictures.

"I'm not worried about your getting work," he said. "You'll always get a job and do it well, because what-ever you do, you put your heart and soul into it. But you'll have your work cut out for you to get the house done before the snow flies."

Leo's wife, as shy and slender as he was stocky and vociferous (though both stood barely five feet tall), worried about how we would live. She knew our sav-ings were limited.

"It's too late to get a garden in," she fretted. "And nobody will give you a job because of all the public-ity." My name had been in the papers frequently in connection with the strike.

"Oh, they'll make out all right," Leo had reassured her, although he, too, knew we had less than $5,000. "I just wish we could go up there, too, and help."

We arrived at the farm on Memorial Day, 1958, in an ancient Nash Ambassador pulling a borrowed trailer that contained our household goods — with a complete set of plumbing tools loaned to me by Leo, with my inevitable canoe atop the car, and with the optimism that comes of youth and good weather.

We pitched our tents in the matted weeds, kicking

tin cans out of the way and trying to be stoic about the mosquitoes. In daylight we began looking around systematically and carefully — the sort of thing sensible people do *before* making a decision, although ours already had been made. The bridges were burned; there was nothing to go back to. All we knew of what lay ahead was that a shelter able to withstand winter had to be created from the ruins around us in the next few weeks. A job and making a living would come after that.

Peonies, honeysuckle, and rugosa roses planted lovingly thirty and forty years before lay buried under mounds of rusting tin cans; we found a receipt dated from the early 1920's amid the heaps of molding, rotting clothes in the house. It showed that carefully saved pennies had been finally dispatched to a seed house for the roses. The sender was the young daughter of the pioneer who founded the farm, and now her dream of loveliness was covered over by the refuse and trash of others' neglect. It would take two years to bring back the roses and honeysuckle from their hardy original roots.

We floundered a few days, thoroughly examined the buildings, and began cleaning up. Demolition of some of the outbuildings would produce only a few usable beams; the rest of the wood was rotten. The barn was partially usable as just that — a barn; the most innovative approaches could not convert it into a home. The best building of the lot was the poultry house, but its shape and structure could turn it into a garage and workshop at best. What was left was the farmhouse (where the roof leaked and the interior was a junk-filled midden) and the unfinished and smaller second house (which had been used as a grain storage place, and then to store fertilizer). We could not possibly start a building anew; there was neither money nor time. Which of the two was it to be?

Should we fix up the granary? It was small but had a sturdy frame on a reinforced-concrete slab which covered a poured-concrete basement. At the bottom was a deep cistern intended as a well until the diggers had been halted by granite. I measured, sketched, considered dormers and built-ons, and tried to solve the problem of dankness and moisture that seemed permanently trapped in the concrete tomb under the house.

Should we repair the main farmhouse? It was a frame structure on cracked concrete footings. Originally two gabled sheds had been moved together at right angles to make the house, and now all structural faults had been compounded by abuse, neglect, and having been open to the elements. It was also filled with heaps and mountains of donated clothing which neighbors had given to the bankrupted last occupants and their many children, and which had been left behind to rot, mildew, and stink to the point where no one could remain in the building long. The odor produced violent nausea.

Bad as it was, the house offered the only practical basis. My oldest son, Smith, and I, wearing kerchiefs over our faces, cleaned it out and we sold the salvageable rags for forty-eight dollars. Then all three boys — Smith, Paul, and Derek — climbed on the roof and began removing half-rotted wooden shingles while I worked behind them and put on a new roof.

The sound of hammering from daybreak until night-fall lured neighbors, who could hear us a mile and more away. They had heard about us and stopped by to visit and encourage us, and while they were all too busy on their farms to help, they did what they could. One of them, on his way to town one day, stopped by with his truck and hauled rags to the junk dealer. On another day he hauled scrap metal. Another stopped by with peony bulbs, explaining: "My mother got the original bulbs from your yard forty years ago, when it was a show place. I thought you might like them, they've spread in my yard and I have more than I need."

While I was handy and somewhat experienced, I had much to learn. From boyhood on I always had to work after school and during summers: bakery helper, farmhand, construction worker, carpenter's helper, printer and pressman, furnace tender in a steel mill, statistician and legal researcher. Now what skills I had acquired stood me in good stead, but they weren't al-ways enough and I made mistakes, such as roofing the house before finishing the basement and framing; usu-ally one fixes and builds walls before the roof. And all of us were careless about tools at first, leaving them about, not keeping them in good repair and sharpened.

At a family council meeting we agreed that anyone leaving a tool about would be fined twenty-five tin cans, which had to be garnered and put in the pile to be disposed of later. None of us at first took the pun-

ishment to be a hardship; after all, there was an endless supply of the cans. But after a week they weren't
all that easy to find, and when Derek called out, "Dad,
you left the sledgehammer next to the silo!" I had to
scrounge and look for a while. And the pile of gathered cans had grown into a mountain.

"Derek, you left the nail puller next to the milk
house!"

"Damn!"

"What?"

"Nothing. I'll pick up cans a little later."

"Now."

Derek was eleven, Paul thirteen, Smith fourteen.
They worked the long days which in our north country
began around five in the morning. Daylight lasted
until nearly ten at night. My wife cooked on a Cole-
man stove, and helped as her time and strength permitted. Soon all of us were engulfed in fatigue, from
which there was no major letup for over four months.

We repaired the exterior frame and siding, and enclosed the screened porch for eventual conversion to a
hallway and bathroom. It was yet another piece of
work done out of sequence, as we found out to our
dismay, and each mistake cost time and effort. We put
in new window sashes and doors, which cost a lot,
despite much shopping around for bargains.

When we gutted the interior of the house we found
that the old kitchen had no running water and no windows. An extensive water system connected the milk
house and the barn, a necessity for the attempt of the
last owner to qualify as a dairy farmer — but his wife

the footing. But each day as I dug, the sand dried out more and caved in. Hour by hour, the cave-in widened. Children and wife helped me tear beams from the condemned outbuildings and prop them under the eaves of the house, angling them out to the ground, in hopes that half the building would not break off and fall into the widening hole. The nightmare turned into disaster as the sugary sand dried, sifted, and rattled into the hole faster than I could shovel it out. Like the sorcerer's apprentice, I was creating a sand mountain next to the house, and making no progress under it. Our dwindling resources had to be tapped to hire help.

A salty old Scandinavian builder and an incredibly strong Indian carpenter joined me in the Black Hole of Calcutta. We shored, propped, planked what we could (praying and joking where we could not put up supports), and shoveled. We had poured the first section of footing for the basement wall, had let it cure the minimum time, and had begun laying blocks, when a crack and a rumble sent us flying out through the gap between excavation and sill of the house. All our supports and props came flying after us like so many arrows, and the half of floor slab I had left behind for bathroom and hall slid into the hole, raising a cloud of dust. But the big beams outside held up the house, floating above the hole. I climbed back in with the sledgehammer and began pounding out the slab. The carpenter took one look at my slashed and bleeding hand, and apparently could relate to both my stoicism and anger: he climbed down and joined me. The builder headed for the chiropractor, and then he came back to help as best he could; he had a back injury that plagued him for over a year afterwards.

After the basement was done and capped, and the floors put in, a stairway had to be built leading to the second floor. I procured a carpenter's handbook from the library and, carefully following the directions, built stairs that turned intricately halfway up, so as to save floorspace downstairs. It was artfully and ingeniously conceived, and would prove to be a conversation piece and an eye-catcher. But when I got ready to fasten the contraption to the downstairs floor and the upstairs header, there was one step too many. It was an amateur mistake, and I had to rebuild the whole thing.

Leo and his family drove up and helped, but his time was limited. We ran out of money and decided to save the interior paneling until the following year. So long as the house was insulated and enclosed, it was only an aesthetic disadvantage; but what a depressing one. Then I discovered a dusty bin of rejected "seconds" of cedar paneling in the lumberyard, where I had become accepted as a bargain hunter and scrounger. They let me have the binful for $100, and I found the sweet wood responsive. Even now the memory of the smell of cedar sawdust evokes a good feeling, and when the paneling was done the house had a honey-colored glow inside. Outside it was painted barn red with white trim by my wife, who overcame her horror of heights to do this essential job.

And suddenly one day the yard was neat, the house trim and ready to move into; and a visitor said: "It looks good, like it used to. Different, but good." He was talking about a time thirty or forty years ago, and he was also telling us that in a rural community where people had been moving away for years, newcomers were welcome.

I took short-term jobs, some of them out of state, to replenish our exhausted funds; the boys began the slow process of making friends and establishing themselves in a new school; we became involved in 4-H, Farmers Union, and township meetings; and we began a series of many meetings with Peter Woodiwiss, the U.S. Agricultural Extension Service forester and adviser, to explore what we could do with the farm to make it productive. He arranged soil tests and generously gave of his time, training, and experience; what's more, he wasn't afraid to take up far-out and seemingly preposterous ideas.

Using an aerial photo of the farm, he helped us identify soil types, principally sand on the high ground and deep peat in the lows. We pinpointed erosion problems, where runoff rain was washing gullies into the fields, and we examined the natural tree stands and brush areas covering about half of the 200 acres for potential income sources. There was much incidental learning on my part: we could plant caragana to hold soil and coincidentally feed wildlife; we could use willow as field dividers and conservation measures. We signed up for a conservation program and ordered 25,000 Norway pine for planting the next spring. It frightened us to think of planting so many trees, and

Peter patiently explained what a planting machine was, how it worked; and he heaped literature on our kitchen table. "I'll be there to help you," he promised, and spring seemed far away. He helped us find a neighboring farmer who cut the hay in the fields, which cleaned them up, though the hay was poor.

The commitment to plant some trees on unused land which we could easily spare did not resolve any questions about what we would do with the farm as a whole. It was just a statement of principle in behalf of conservation — a vote of thanks to the land for having us — and our many meetings devoted to the search for a plan for the farm continued.

Then winter came in earnest. The car wouldn't start, signifying that we had new skills to learn about coping with cold and the dangers of sub-zero living. A car could slide off the ice on the road and, on our sparsely traveled roads, might not be discovered for many hours; and one could freeze to death quickly, drifting into an easy and perpetual sleep.

But the first winter crisis was brought on not by one of the obvious dangers, nor by my ineptness at automobile mechanics and maintenance. It was caused by my early decision to get by with the outdoor privy until spring. We had water in the house, and I had installed all the plumbing myself; but we were short of cash and decided to be hardy in the matter of the toilet.

As it got colder, we would delay and procrastinate going outside until it was no longer a matter of choice.

I would bundle up, plunge outdoors, and not resume breathing until I was in the privy, which provided the illusion of shelter. But as soon as I dropped my pants and lifted the lid, winds from all points of the compass came roaring through the hole in the bench. I completed the installation of a toilet before December.

As the long and bitter winter began to wane, the discussions with Peter began to take form and a pattern emerged — most of our notions and dreams would not work out or were far beyond our means. We made a partial inventory of the farm uses we had considered:

Domesticated blueberries — Soil not suitable, climate too rigorous, cost of establishment too high for us.

Wild rice — Creation of paddies beyond our means, nonshattering seed strains are not in existence. The only experiment in paddy culture is still very young and shows no prospects of breaking even in the next few years; it is being conducted by a wealthy individual at a site fifty miles north of us. Wisconsin experiments in seeding and harvesting in natural lakes where water level and water chemistry are closely controlled are not working out. Buying and selling rice and going into marketing is already highly competitive, requires starter capital we don't have.

Truck farming — Zucchini, carrots, squash do well but demand is limited. We are far from canneries and bulk buyers. Most big food firms raise their own or contract with suppliers.

Peat production — Lots of peat, one of the richest sources of pure organic matter. But the humic acid releases this storehouse of nitrogen, potash, etc., too slowly to be of value to farmers, and the chemical research into obtaining a quicker release is beyond our capabilities. Market demand for plain dried peat is limited, considering our restricted means to buy heavy equipment, go into marketing.

We could augment subsistence by *gardening* and raising some *livestock*, such as pigs, sheep, chickens, ducks, perhaps one or two head of cattle a year.

Tree farming seemed to be the only practical and realistic use of the land, Peter thought, and the idea had to grow on me for a while. It could furnish a steady, if modest, income once I retired, but I would have to find work in town or elsewhere in the meantime, making of the farm a home and a way of life, and gradually a producing tree farm.

It was a strange notion to speak of growing trees as a means of livelihood — they grow so slowly. I was a little embarrassed explaining it to friends at first, laughing it off by saying, "Well, we're doing it for aesthetic reasons." Or "for environmental" or "ecological" purposes. These were all true, but not the real nub of it.

"In five or six years you can sell Christmas trees," Peter said, while I dubiously nodded my head. "In fifteen to twenty years you will have to thin the plantation again, which will give you income from selling posts and poles."

"Yes, that's right," I said, but my heart wasn't in it. It didn't seem real. I didn't know how I was going to plant all those trees next spring, much less think about cutting them. Twenty years! How'll I manage two months from now?

But Peter was relentless. "There are some big trees

out there that were damaged by lightning and by fires long ago. If you don't harvest them, a wind will blow them over. This is income, and you can replant."

What he said was true, but I was repelled by the idea of cutting those beautiful big trees. I couldn't visualize seedlings to be planted in a few weeks becoming big, changing the landscape, altering the ecological and wildlife patterns. But slowly, patiently, we drew up the long-range plan for the tree farm in color-coded overlays on the old aerial photo of the land: Old field to be planted in 1959, 25,000 trees; old pasture to be planted in 1960, 40,000 trees; small field to be planted in 1961, 35,000 trees. . . . Erosion point, to be planted in caragana. . . . Wildlife area, to be planted in caragana and willow. . . . Natural stand to be pruned, selectively cut, and spot-planted. . . . Scrub aspen and jack pine, natural regeneration, to be harvested and planted in Norway pine. . . .

It was a thick file folder when we were done, and seemed a bit foolish and presumptuous to me, who had only seen pictures of a planting machine.

We didn't give up on the other farm-use ideas all at once, but they disappeared. "Did you look into bee-keeping a little more?" Peter would ask. "I don't know much about that."

"It's all right for subsistence, but doubtful commercially. In this climate you have to winter-feed the colony, which reduces the amount of honey you can take by about half. Or you kill off the bees in the fall, and restock from a supply house in spring, which cuts down on the time they have to multiply and collect honey." (I'd helped my father keep bees when I was young, and had written to some experts for information.)

Another time I raised the prospect of musk oxen. They were being domesticated for their long-fibered wool, but it turned out that there were few available; that they would have to be carefully fenced, which represented a major outlay; and that the commercial outlets for the wool were then nonexistent. But I fantasized about musk oxen roaming around the farm in the willow marshes that they would like, and in a climate they would find comfortable. It was one of many notions I did not discuss with my neighbors, who thought me peculiar enough as it was when I talked about tree farming, though they still welcomed us.

"Too bad maple trees are such slow growers," I said to Peter during one of our final sessions. "It'd be nice to be able to make your own syrup, and the one patch of field you marked on the map has heavy enough soil for them to grow." I was learning.

"Why don't you put in a few?" Peter responded. "In a couple hundred years your great-grandchildren can tap them."

Two hundred years? Twenty years? I had to start making plans for two months hence when I would need a tractor, gas, oil, grease, a rented planting machine, and seedlings. Would I have to hire help or could we do it ourselves? How long would it take to plant 25,000 trees?

But the time came, and Peter was there to get us started. He arrived concurrently with the returning red-winged blackbirds and the hawks, the first week in May. He brought the bundles from Badoura State Nursery, and had the tree-planting machine hooked to his pickup truck. I had meanwhile picked up a small tractor at an auction and had painstakingly accumulated the other items Peter thought I might need: old milk cans to haul water, a grease gun and bulk grease for the planter, extra gas and oil for the tractor, an extra hitch for pulling the planter, burlap bags to put on the hard metal seats of the planter.

Peter opened the first bundle with pliers, showed us how to separate the seedlings whose roots were intertwined from being bundled, and how to put them in water buckets wired to the planter. Smith drove the tractor while my wife and I planted the hill between the lakes, Peter walking behind giving advice:

"Hold on to the seedlings a little longer . . . wait for the tug of the moving machine to pull it out of your hand . . . space them better." They were to be six feet apart; some planting machines have a bell that rings at preset intervals denoting planting distances, but this machine was mute.

"Drive faster," Peter advised, and the machine bumped and heaved, the furrows opening and closing, gapingly demanding to be fed seedlings. The tempo of the work overcame my nervousness. Then there was no more advice from Peter. I looked up from the planting and saw him standing a hundred feet away on the lake trail, heading back to the farmstead.

"Where are you going?" I yelled to him.

"Got work to do. You're doing all right."

"I thought you were going to help!"

"I did. Now you know all I do. Good luck!" He was gone and I felt alone and nervous again, but the machine kept moving and I had to keep planting.

We had trouble with the tractor, which was too small and light to do the job properly; the tree count was off and we planted nearly forty thousand; the packing mechanism on the planter had to be adjusted to eliminate air pockets around the roots of the seedlings, which could kill the trees. We learned to pace ourselves and how much we could do in a day; our first planting was done in three days. Over the years we learned about tree species and their relationships and uses, of the dominance of jack pine over popple, of Norway over jack pine. We learned painfully, slowly, about hand-planting, and to know the soil and the weather, to treasure wet springs and thunderstorms, to dread the stretches of drought. Over the years we have planted about two hundred thousand trees, and each time when we start my heart skips a beat as it did the first time, when I became a tree farmer, and *the* farm became the *tree* farm.

3

The Forever Tree

DAVID IS FIVE and wants to plant a "forebber" tree.
"What's a forever tree?"

"My own tree," he explains. I think he means an alter ego whose life and fortunes would betoken his own. It's an old idea, imbedded in legend and mythology from prehistoric times. I'm inclined against magic and superstition, and consider it risky to identify one's life with the vicissitudes that can beset a single tree.

"You've helped me plant lots of trees. Why do you want your own?"

"It'll be my own and it'll be here forebber and ebber, like our farm."

There it was: primitive man looking for eternal life by tying it symbolically to a tree. I suppose he'll want a pine tree yet, an evergreen which confounds the passage of the seasons by staying perpetually green. Yet how does one cope with a child's wishes?

"Next spring we'll have a big planting. Your older brothers, Smith, Paul, and Derek, will be coming home to help. And you can plant lots of trees then."

"I want to plant my forebber tree right now."

"Tomorrow we'll be working in the plantation and you can plant some then." I was studiously avoiding the single-tree notion.

"One's enough, Daddy."

Maybe for all my fussing about primitive mythology and superstition, I'm not all that far removed from David's outlook. Peggy says I just operate on a larger scale.

We roll up old fence, though by now there is not much left. I like the feeling of easy transition into a forest and want others to be able to enjoy this also, whether they are passing by on the sand road that bisects the tree farm or whether they are on foot and want to walk about. In some Scandinavian countries all forests, even privately or corporately owned, are considered public domain for purposes of walking, picnicking, or camping. I tend to agree with this and see the justice of it; nature is here for all of us, despite the happenstance of temporary private ownership. But I am also aware, sometimes painfully so, that this public access brings with it occasional irresponsible and thoughtless acts, such as the taking of Christmas trees — often from the worst places, where there are already gaps in the plantation or erosion problems — or wanton damage. And inevitably there is litter, a residue of cans and wrappers, that I doubt one would find in Scandinavia.

At any rate, we are still removing old fences. It's a job we've been at, off and on during spare time, since the first year. Initially we'd taken down most of the dividing fences between fields but left the ones along the county road. As the plantation trees got bigger, we had taken down major sections of that as well. Now there are only odd little lots and fields left enclosed, with fences that are overgrown by brush and scrub. This fencing is hard to untangle, and I have a healthy respect for rusty barbed wire. It springs and snaps, and there are scratches despite work gloves and caution. It's a job the young boys have to watch from a distance.

"What do you do with it?" David still asks questions to which he knows the answers, particularly when he has to stand forty feet away and wants attention. He also may be trying to protect his vested interest in the promised planting of his "forebber" tree.

"I put it in the washout, the gully."

"Why?"

"It helps to stop the soil from washing away. Plants grow over it."

"Why are you taking it down?"

"It's no use here and it's some use there. Also people trip over it and can hurt themselves."

"Like you did when you cut your leg?"

"Yes." This job tends to make me ill-tempered and irascible. I wish David would play at the sandpile or the creek, but he is drawn to me by the prohibition against coming closer.

"Daddy, can we measure candles?" Tony asks. He's

been playing with pinecones. He and David have very different personalities. Tony can always find something interesting to do and become involved in, while David needs companionship. It's not a factor of ages, of the older child's having had independence, while the younger always had a brother for playmate. I think it was conditioned more by David's early-childhood illness, which made us overprotective. Long after he was robust and vigorous I still tended to react protectively to his demands and thereby gave impetus to a personality trait.

"We measured candles yesterday," I tell Tony.

"Can we do it today?" It's Tony's way of telling me that I've worked long enough and that he is due for some attention too, despite his generally independent nature.

"Okay, when I finished the fence here."

Candles are what we call the new spring growth on the pine, the projections that look like flexible, finger-like white candles at the end of the branches. With time their white down covering turns into pale-green feathery needles. As the needles elongate they become darker green. When seedlings are first planted the candles are very short and it may take several years before the growth rate goes to a foot or more a year. Well-established trees can produce candles averaging twelve to fifteen inches or longer, and in good growing years they can be three feet or longer among the top branches. It's unnecessary to measure them except as a means of making the idea of growth a reality to the young boys.

The old wire has lost some of its pliability and is difficult to manage. It is hot out, and the sweat is running into my eyes. This is the time to be particularly careful, when impatience and discomfort are upon me. I have no desire to have a strand of the stuff spring into my face or slash my arm such as happened in earlier years, when I had been at the start of my learning curve. The last strand is on the ground now, disconnected from the rotting posts, and I start the first loop of the roll, which will be about two feet in diameter. I crisscross the strand on the ground with the growing roll, and finally twist the loose end around the roll several times to lock it together. It is a tight roll and I heave it on the truck, the job done for the day. Then we measure candles on a few nearby plantation trees, and finally sit down in the cool shade of an overhanging spruce in an older, natural grove of trees near the hilltop.

Across the lake Peggy emerges on the path leading from the house, heading for a stroll around the lake. Seventy or eighty feet ahead of her a doe steps from the bushes, sniffs the air, and ambles down the same path my wife will follow. She cannot see the deer but I see her bend to examine the ground and then resume her walk.

"Can you boys be very quiet if I tell you something?"

"Sure. What?"

"Look across the lake. See your mother over there? No, *don't* call her, David. Now look ahead of her on the path around the lake. See anything?"

They both peer. Then Tony smiles as he sees the

deer. Moments later David says: "I see it, it's a deer. D'you see it, Tony?" Tony nods, still smiling, and "shhhs" his brother. I'd hoped the deer would walk out in front of us but it takes a turn, crosses behind us, and fades into the woods. A few minutes later Peggy joins us with a pitcher of lemonade. She had noticed the deer tracks but had not seen the deer. The boys enjoy lording it over their mother and Peggy graciously plays their game. Then Tony brags about the size of the candles we measured.

"Our tree farm has always been here and will be forebber and ebber." David is given to superlatives.

"The tree farm was started by your father over seventeen years ago," Peggy answers. "And it took a lot of work to bring it this far."

"That's a long time," Tony observes.

"Long before you and David were born."

I think of the years and the beginnings, and also of the "forever and ever" all children and adults long for. One can't very well caution young children that fires, drought, tornadoes, or disease can wipe out a tree farm; that unexpected events can change and turn lives, societies, and nations. Who could have planned one's life on the expectation of an atom bomb? Of a Vietnam? Who can plant trees and expect to see a mature forest, much less know what will happen to the seedlings on a journey longer than one's own? To children in search of absolute security the formula "it has always been and always will be" is necessary.

No one knows what will befall the course of one's life, much less what will happen to the seeds one sows — to the children or to the trees one tends. But it is patently unfair to pretend, even to young children, that anything in life "always has been and will be."

"Once this was virgin forest," I tell them. "In places there were only large trees which had crowded out all underbrush. You could walk on a floor of pine needles for great distances. Indian runners could travel from one encampment to the other, and among the old men today there are some who can still remember how it was.

"Indians lived here for many thousands of years. There were different tribes, as cultures and civilizations came and went and as the people migrated. But all Indians who lived here, and hunted and harvested wild rice, and berries, and vegetables, lived as part of the land and the forest, and left it as they found it, undamaged and unchanged."

"We are Indians," Tony says solemnly, and David nods agreement. The boys' multicultural origins are a frequent source of pride and strength to them, and only occasionally result in confusion about what is Jewish, what is Indian, and what as a consequence they should think themselves to be.

"We are Chippewa Indians," David reinforces. The word *Chippewa* is commonly used, a corruption of *Ojibwe,* though the Indian word is *Ahnishinabe,* or *Shinabe* in the vernacular.

"That's right, David," I tell him. "And the Chippewas lived here for about two hundred years. And before them the Sioux lived here, and before them the Middle Mississippians and the mound builders." I have learned to anticipate David's questions, but not all of them.

"Where did the Chippewas live before they came here?"

"They came from the east, all along the Great Lakes to Lake Superior and then inland. Anyhow, when the Europeans came to settle here, they took the land —"

"How could they take the land from the Indians?"

"Well, Indians believed that land did not 'belong' to anybody, that a person just used it while they lived. So the idea of buying or selling land seemed foolish to them. And when white people first showed up and wanted treaties signed that gave away land, the Indians tried to humor them. Some of the Indians in those days did not want to embarrass the white people by telling them that you could not buy or sell land that belonged to all creation.

"Then the whites took over land, and there was less space for the Indians. Finally soldiers were brought in and reservations were set up for the Indians, and the rest of the land taken over by the whites."

"That wasn't right!" the boys protest.

"It wasn't, and isn't, and both your mother and I try to do something about it."

"Did the Indians and the soldiers fight?"

"Not very much around here, but the last battle between Indians and the U.S. Army was fought a little ways from here at Sugar Point on Leech Lake. That was around 1898."

"Who won?"

"The Indians won the battle but the whites won the

war. Through treaties and military as well as economic
force, the bulk of the land here was taken away, and
what remained to the Indians was parceled, divided,
until now less than 20 percent of the reservation is still
owned by Indians individually or tribally. The land of
our farm was taken by the U.S. government when the
Leech Lake Reservation boundary was established by
treaty. Then the land was turned over to the state of
Minnesota, and they turned it over to railroad and
timber companies, which moved in and cut the big
trees so the lumber could be used to build the cities of
middle America. People came from faraway countries
to work as loggers, many from Scandinavia. And some
of those loggers stayed behind after the timber was cut
and the companies moved to other forests, and those
who stayed made farms of the land. They worked hard
digging out tree stumps and carving drainage ditches
with oxen teams. The drainage ditches on our farm
were over a quarter mile long, and lined with tamarack planks. . . ."

Often the early farmers would leave wives and children to work the farms while they hired themselves
out during the grain harvests farther west. Evidently
they hoped that the cash they brought home combined
with the proceeds of the farm would help them turn
the corner. But the corner was elusive, as is indicated
by the property abstracts and titles filed in the county
courthouse. As soon as one mortgage was paid up, another loan had to be taken out. Our own abstract and
title shows many such transactions, and that our farm

was owned continuously by one family from the first platting in 1900 until 1940's.

The pioneering parents who first settled on our land intended to have one of their children take over the house and farm, and they started to build a second, or "parents' house," but it was not completed once it was enclosed. (The inexorable grind of human generations does not always go as expected.) There were disease and death, setbacks and disappointments. Of the three brothers who pioneered three adjoining farms, only one founded a farm that still remained in operation fifty years later.

It is one of the two formerly unsuccessful farms that is now ours. Descendants of the pioneer sold it to a returning World War II veteran who had dreams of making it into a dairy farm; he had a large family — twelve children, I was told — but after a few years' efforts he had to give up. The livestock and machinery were sold at auction to satisfy debts and the farm stood idle for some years until we bought it in 1958.

Our life on the tree farm brought my sons and me closer together, but it failed to build a more wholesome first marriage. All partners bring problems to an intimate relationship, and often create more over the years. One needs skills, knowledge, respect, the ability to love and to be loved. And I think we both lacked skills, and dwelt too much on the past and not enough on the goodness of *right now*. Sadly, it came to an end some time after the older boys had grown and left the tree farm.

And now my second marriage, my younger sons . . . Had I become a better person, more cognizant of my character and therefore a better partner and parent?

"Daddy, let's plant some trees right now! I don't want to wait until next spring!" Right now. Here and now.

We get the spade and pick four trees from crowded clumps in the woods, one from each of us as a present to the others: a balsam — flat-needled, compact; a cedar — sweet-smelling, sinuous; a white pine — its feather needles soft and supple; and a little birch — the bark brown with fawn's spots (it would turn white in a few years). We plant along the bank of the creek where Tony and David play. Where someday their children would play? . . .

"This is my forebber tree," David says.

"And this one is mine," Tony proclaims.

And mine, and mine, for Peggy, for Smith and Paul and Derek, for my father and mother, and grandchildren . . .

"Next spring we'll plant ten thousand," I say.

"Forebber trees?"

"Pine and spruce."

Trees, like all living things, have a life cycle and die. There are no forever trees. It is only the process of planting, of affirming life, that has the potential, the connotation, of forever. David will work this out for himself in his own way as he grows up and matures. We all do.

4

4

Planting

THE FROST IS OUT of the ground and Badoura State Nursery will start pulling two-year-old seedlings from the beds next week. It is extraordinary that it is May; usually it is April when the annual season begins. For the first time in several years all of my older sons will be coming home for planting. I wrote them each, setting out the particulars and making final arrangements. Derek is in Minneapolis, completing a documentary movie on life as perceived by a severely cerebral-palsied person; he and his wife are planning to come and help, and to take some movies, providing their present filming is completed. Smith will leave his handcraft studio, east of Minneapolis. Paul and his bride, Mary, who has never seen a big planting before, will drive over from Duluth, where his medical school is having a three-day weekend. Tony and David have visions of driving the tractor, but they'll have to wait a

few years. Driving a tree-planting rig is as hard as plowing (harder, I say, but this is an unresolved argument).
As a rule we plant the first week in May. Badoura
starts pulling sometime in April and delivers to the
southern townships first, working north in pursuit of
the receding frost line. Since we are pretty far north, it
gets to be our turn three weeks into the season or later.

I often walk where the first planting took place, taking pride in the twenty-foot-high Norway pines. It
seems whenever I go for a walk I somehow find my
way home through that section of first planting, no
matter how out of the way. The ground is full of prints
I wouldn't have seen the first year: deer, fox, raccoon.
There are dens and beds among the pine duff and grass.

Planting-time weather is quirky; it's the time of year
for sudden changes. The old journal says that in 1959,
on May 5 we had a high of ninety-one degrees and a
low of forty-two degrees. The year 1960 was not quite
so warm, and usually the highs in May were around
fifty-five degrees — with a couple of exceptions, when
it sleeted and didn't get above thirty-five degrees.

I called the county extension office and a new man
there reserved the planting machine for me. Did I
want the small one or the big one with the scalpers?
The small one, I told him, since the sod was fairly thin
on my sandy soil and not too much competition for the
little trees. It didn't warrant scalping back the grass.
Besides, the scalping releases dormant weed seeds.
The fellow wasn't too interested and he seemed a little
impatient. Amusing, because when I started tree farming the extension service had a full-time forester who

indoctrinated me; I was just trying to return the favor. Now there was no longer any forester at all on the staff. It seems to me I had been a more enthusiastic pupil, but then growing trees isn't everyone's passion.

Speaking of which, Carl Olson stopped me in the hardware store, saying he had driven by the other day and that the east planting "sure is pretty." Once he had commented acidly — I think it was the second or third year — that his uncle had cleared that land by hand, with a team of oxen to pull stumps; he was implying that it was a crime to plant trees and negate the pioneers' efforts. Some others in the township felt the same. I think now that Carl is older and not farming so intensively, he's become more reflective. He finds the soil being leached, used up beyond the capability of commercial fertilizer to replace nutrients economically. Maybe he's concluded that the trees have a place in nature and in the cycle of life, and are not just the ancient obstacles his immigrant father and uncles grubbed out after cutting the virgin timber at the turn of the century. Anyhow — whatever the reason — I'm glad he said it. And I hope my suggestion to him a few years ago about hauling peat out of the marsh and disking it into his field continues to work. The peat is pure organic matter with slow-release humic acid containing phosphate, nitrogen, potash, and minerals the soil needs. It holds moisture, too. He tried it on his small pasture and stitched rye and Sudan grass seed into the alfalfa. The pasture looks good.

Pileated woodpeckers are back; I heard them today

but didn't see them. A red-tailed hawk was circling overhead whistling his hunting cry; I hope they nest in the big spruce overlooking the swamp again. Seven deer beds on the south hill and a brush wolf track along the lake. The loons were crying at sunset; how I long for that sound during winter; how it touches my soul.

We have a date certain now. We will pick up trees on Friday the twenty-fourth in late afternoon. The same day we'll pick up the planting machine, the planting bars from State Forestry, gas and oil; check the tractor; double-check on the hand-planting crew. Then we'll have the three-day Memorial Day weekend. Rain or shine we'll have to plant on Saturday, Sunday, and Monday. Somebody else has the machine reserved for Tuesday. And State Forestry was plainspoken about it: I could have all the planting bars I wanted for the hand-planters for the long weekend, but I had to have them back by 8 A.M. Tuesday because that day they had scheduled a big crew to replant a burned-over stretch, and they would need every bar early in the morning, if not the night before.

Badoura said the bundles might be heavier this year, meaning either bigger seedlings or an overage of trees to compensate for poor or small stock. There are 500 trees to a bundle this year. A few years ago, during the Eisenhower soil-bank time, the demand was so great that the 2-0 stock of pine was puny, and bundles of "1,000" often had nearly 2,000 tiny trees. We planted pretty close together then, with five-foot intervals between trees on the assumption they weren't as hardy and we would lose more. As the stock got better, we could space them out more. The assumption had been correct. Scuttlebutt: bundles this year run at 50 percent overage and the stock is uneven.

I've always wished I could afford the luxury of 2-2 stock: two years in seedbeds, then separated and replanted in nursery beds for another two years. The seedlings aren't much bigger, still only four or five inches above the ground; but the roots are much stronger and sturdier, and the hair roots more plentiful. It's the hair roots that make the difference — that tiny, filigreed system of life.

We played whist with neighbors last night. Old Mr. Hansen and Grandma Amster were partners. He still promises to recollect the great Hinckley forest fire for me — when he was young and rode the last train of escapees through the blistering heat. Today he was out planting by hand, his arms moving in great arcs spreading oats — and always on the same 4 acres; his son farms the remaining 156 acres with tractor and machines, but the man now nearing ninety reserves the hand-planting of that small patch for himself. It is beautiful watching him, because his entire body is given to the ancient ritual, and his rhythm as he walks and sows is an act of love. Now, as he plays whist, there is a secret smile that flits over his face, and I think it has to do with his winning again. Grandma Amster doesn't smile during the play of a hand, but

when it's done her wrinkled face will split in a rictus
and the few remaining yellowed teeth will show.
Wouldn't I like to beat them just once!

The mailman was kind today, bringing confirmation
from Paul and Mary, which makes me particularly
happy because she is so warm and sharing and satisfies
my wishes for a daughter; also she is a hard worker.
Smith wrote in his usual cryptic style, but the message
was good no matter how brief: he will be here.

I walked the long strip aside the east fence, half a
mile long, sixty feet wide, where we'll machine-plant
the spruce. It is a gamble whether the spruce will do
well here, but we will chance it, hoping for moisture
and good growing weather. The sod is thick enough to
have choked out the weeds, and we'll have to set the
planting mechanism deep to get the hair roots below
sod level. I have second thoughts about getting the
machine with the scalper, but it's too late now. Over
across the road where we cut pulpwood last fall the
hand-planting crew will have rough going. There is
more slash on the ground than I'd remembered,
though at the time I thought we'd done right to wind-
row the slashings, dragging the cut-off branches away
and piling them in long parallel rows twenty feet
apart. The idea was good, but the execution left something to be desired. Windrows protect the little trees;
as the slashings decompose and disappear they feed
and nourish the new growth. Today it didn't look as
clean and neat as I'd remembered it. I decided to work

with the hand-planters and leave the machine-planting to Smith, Paul, and Derek. They'd done it often enough when in high school, and would need no telling from me.

I looked for the early flowers and searched in vain for leaves of the fringed gentian, which would not bloom until August. I must prevail on Myrtle Bridgman to take yet another walk with me; she is over seventy and shames me with her endurance, but she knows all the flowers, the local archeology, and which plants produce the native dyes — and she is a national authority on weaving. Where had she found the wild orchids on one of our walks last year — was it along the creek or in the swamp?

Past experience should have warned me, but I am the eternal optimist — a veritable Candide — in that each year I think that tree planting will go smoothly. My notes to myself from previous nights before planting should have prepared me for daylong disaster. When will I learn to accept this as a day when Murphy's Law is automatically invoked? When "anything that can go wrong will go wrong"?

There were no planting bars waiting for me at the forestry station, they had been given to the Girl Scouts for a half-day ceremony somewhere — the duty man didn't know where. But he did know they wouldn't be back until Tuesday. I had visions of an eight-man hand-planting crew next morning without planting bars. There followed a complicated trade-off with Forestry: since I had to drive to Badoura to pick up seedlings I would pass Guthrie Forestry Station on my way; Guthrie happened to have extra planting bars; Guthrie also happened to have some pinecones ready for delivery to Badoura for extraction of seeds. If I could save the Guthrie folks the trip to Badoura, they might let me have the bars. . . . The forestry radio network buzzed and crackled between Guthrie, Badoura, and Bemidji. Joe was out to lunch and Ned didn't know. . . . Two hours and several thimblefuls of adrenalin later, I'm on my way.

At Guthrie *thirty* planting bars are waiting for me. "But I only need ten!" "Well, Bemidji said to give you all I got and that's thirty, and I want you to sign for them." I sign, then load the bars and the sacks of cones. Badoura, next stop.

At Badoura the pace is frenetic. Forestry and private vehicles of every description are pulling in and out on tight schedules. By the time it is my turn as a "northerner," the crews are nearing the end of the spring pulling season, which lasts less than two months. The seasonal help is made up of farmers' wives, a few farmers, and some young men. Stress lines show around their eyes, and some of them have splotchy skin reflecting fatigue and work under constant pressure: pickups are tightly scheduled; some of the drivers come from far away. My own pickup distance is less than a hundred miles one way; all of us try to make the round trip in a day, so that the seedlings will not suffer damage in transit. They must not dry out or overheat.

In three days or so I'll probably look as tired as the

Badoura workers, but I rarely have time to examine myself in the mirror at tree-planting time. My order is ready and waiting for me and I am in and out in fifteen minutes, sandwiched between a leased flatbed trailer hauling 100,000 pine for Forestry and a little pickup there for the first time getting two bundles. My order this year is small by Badoura standards: 5,000 Norway pine and 5,000 spruce. I leave the huge nursery, which is the solitary establishment in miles of lake and pine-tree country. A few miles up the road are scattered fields, then the crossroads town of Akeley, which has a little coffee shop with the best homemade pies in seventeen counties. I stop there each time.

Murphy's Law blinks at my passing Badoura and Akeley, but is with me again in Bemidji when I try to pick up the planting machine. I find it parked next to the country garage Cyclone fence but can't budge it to hitch to my truck's bumper for the ten-mile haul to the farm. I finally lure some help from the garage and with considerable effort we clear the fence, jack and hook the machine. The heavy weights are missing and we will have to jury-rig tomorrow or the planting mechanism won't ride deeply enough — the furrows would be too shallow to set the tree roots properly.

The last straw — when I go to pick up the tractor, neighbor Chuck says: "Oh, tomorrow the day? I'll have to see if it's running. Had some trouble with it a while back and haven't used it since."

Paul and Mary, and Derek, have arrived during my absence. Derek's wife, Elissa, was detained in the Cities at the last minute. I have help now in storing tree

bundles in a moist, cool place, in greasing and checking the planter. The tractor comes chugging down the
drive and we hook up, fasten the buckets that will
carry seedlings, and check and double-check all details
that, unattended, could cost critical time during planting: tools at hand for machine repair; extra oil, gas,
and hydraulic fluid; water cans for seedlings and for
seeders. It goes easier now.

We play whist and pop corn on the wood-burning
range. Some of the tension is residual, but it is mixed
now with anticipaton of the morrow and the fellow-
ship of family. Then Smith arrives, late in the evening;
the little ones hear the racket and get up, and it's a
little raucous and warm; the house glows and smells of
woodsmoke, popcorn, and cocoa. Outside, the moon is
big through the giant picture windows we made of
salvaged plate glass.

It is overcast and heavy dew beads the grass blades,
leaves, and pine needles. It is forty degrees and supposed to go to fifty degrees. The two bucket seats on
the planter are sopping wet and everything is cold to
touch. There is no sign of the hand-planting crew; we
load spruce bundles, water, and extra fuel, start the
tractor, and the caravan is off. All spruce will be
machine-planted on the half-mile stretch along the
fence; the pine will be hand-planted in the cutover *if*
the hand-planting crew shows up.

The excitement of lining up the planter for the first
run! The wonderful pungent smell of peat moss bursts
forth when the first bundle is opened. The aroma curls

up your nose and stays with you all day. The roots are moist, black and orange, about twenty-five trees in a sub-bundle, wrapped in moss; then another twenty-five, heading the other way; tops to the outside of the bundle, roots to the middle to retain moisture. We separate trees and set them upright in pails wired to the planting machine — one pail in front of each bucket seat — and the seedlings are wetted down again. By day's end we'll be less ceremonious but still careful about pulling apart the bundles. Mary is getting her first indoctrination, helping me separate trees. Paul fusses with the tractor, getting unsolicited advice from Derek, and Smith is admiring the older planting to our right; he had driven the rig for that early planting, now nearly twenty feet high, while Paul and I had sat on the planter. Derek had been too small that year. Now the older boys are taller than I am, and David and Tony are running around excitedly.

We've rigged the planter to ride nine inches into the ground. The huge coulter wheel cuts the sod and earth; behind it the shoe plow opens a furrow four inches wide and nine inches deep. I explain to Mary that she and I will be sitting alongside the opening furrow, setting in the seedlings. Underneath us the slanted packing wheels will push the loose earth back around the roots and pack it. That's why the weights are needed.

"As the rig moves, the packing wheels pull the trees out of your hand," I tell her. (She has the first dirt smudges on her face and is excited.) "I'll plant the first row and show you. You sit next to me and separate trees. Pull them apart and hand them to me. About fifteen at a time."

The machine starts with a jerk and nestles into the soil. The furrow opens up between us. I hold the seedlings by the stem, set them in the furrow at a slight angle — tops up and roots down — by feeding them into a metal guide chute that funnels them into the furrow. The packing wheels and the motion of the rig pull the trees out of my hand gently. I hold until I feel the set of the tree, until I can feel it anchoring into the ground, and for an instant there is physical bond between man, tree, and earth. First one tree, then the next, and the next; behind us the thin brown line stretches out, the tiny tree tufts peeking out and waving at the sky.

The earth is moist and dark, cold to the touch. I savor the little plants, the living roots, the open rich soil, and wish the plants well on their journey into time. I glance to our right at the first planting, now fifteen years old. It had not been futile, although sometimes we had wondered. On my left, some sixty feet away, is my neighbor's fence line: piles of stone labored out of the fields, then jack pine and willow planted by hand over the many years by the man and his father. The tractor putts along at a steady pace, the rhythm established. As my hands empty, Mary passes over another handful of seedlings, and we share the bond. Ritual. Thoughts of the Golden Bough.

"Am I doing this right?" I nod, because it's all right and I don't feel like talking. Already birds circle, following the furrow, feeding on grubs, coming closer to the rig: red-winged blackbirds, robins, cowbirds, bob-olinks, crows.

The machine stopped. I looked up in annoyance, wishing to go on. We were at the end of the run, up against the fence line, and the rig had to turn around. We got off the bucket seats; I pumped up the hydraulic jack, lifting coulter wheel and shoe plow out of the ground. We stretched, brushed dirt and wet moss from our pants, looked at each other and smiled.

Mary planted the next run; I separated trees for her — my turn to get cold, wrinkled hands from handling the wet seedlings while she got the feel of the moist, gritty soil brushing against her hands. Where the land lay low the earth gave off cool breaths like puffs of icy winter winds as the furrows opened and closed, reminders of the great cold of winter that was and would be again. Something about the planting and nurture of trees evokes the pattern of the year, and of the years: of the growth of my children and now theirs; of the pattern of our lives and our loving. I looked over at my new daughter Mary, so intent and no longer worried whether she was doing it "right," involved now and following the train of her thoughts. The sun came out and made Mary's red hair glisten, highlighting the smudges on her face. I'm glad my son brought such a warm, loving woman into the family. The machine stopped again, to turn around where we had begun over half an hour ago (although it seemed but moments ago, with the earth and seedlings gliding through our hands). We had planted two rows, each half a mile long; and the earth had revolved a bit on its axis, and was a bit better for the hope of the trees. It was going too fast — we would be done in a day or two — and it seemed only moments ago that I had been a small child and had stood beside my father as he grafted fruit trees.

The youngest boys were waiting with a message, clamoring: "Come on, Daddy. The men are here to help plant the trees!" But we did part of another row, each of the little ones taking a turn on my lap, getting the first feel of this kind of bond with the earth. One more glance at the new furrows, six feet apart — at the tiny seedlings marching into the future in straight lines at seven-foot intervals. I knew they would lose that well-kempt look before long. Drought, disease, and the shock of transplanting would kill at least 10 percent — leaving gaps and open spaces.

I met the crew and passed out the steel planting bars, each sharpened to a good cutting edge at the four-inch base. We shouldered the heavy bundles for the quarter-mile hike to the planting site. "Plant them tight," I admonished. "Step them in. No air pockets around the roots." The crew consisted of the high school counselor, an old friend and planting partner; three students; and several men who work for Forestry on weekdays. We spread out in a line between the first windrows of slashings and began. Occasionally we could hear the machine in the distance; it can plant 1,000 an hour, if all goes well. One of us, in good condition, on clear, easy ground can hand-plant 800 a day. Today was not going to be an 800 day — that was plain from the start. The soil was hard, some of the men still soft, and the terrain was jumbled with branches, roots, and slashings.

I like to plant with a rhythm: Stride. Plunge bar in ground. Rock back and forth to make the wedge-shaped opening. Pull bar, slide seedling in hole, and pull up and down to seat hair roots. Plunge bar into ground two inches behind seedling, rock back and forth to pack. Step-in the newly planted seedling — left side, right side. Stride and plunge.

By late morning progress was slow. Peggy brought lunch and coffee and word that the tractor had broken down but was being fixed. Above us the sun was strong and hot, and I had a growing concern the trees might dry out: dry, dead hair roots mean a dead tree. We put the bundles in the little creek, sheltered by an over-hanging tree.

I ate fast and headed back to the machine-planting, on the way tugging at the hand-planted tree tufts to check for firm packing. One day they would tower. . . . But the first one I checked would never tower over anything — it came out of the ground when I pulled it. So did the next one.

"Who planted this row?"

"Which one?"

"Second one up."

The planter was one of three high school students.

"Look, son, you're planting dead trees. The air pocket around the roots will kill that tree. Here's what you do to pack rightly. This is how you step it in. Don't step over the tree, step right next to it. Both sides." We did a few trees together, retracing his steps. The other rows were better. A nice-looking, strong boy. But he didn't seem to care much about trees, though he was willing enough to work. Peggy didn't say anything, but after packing up lunch she took a planting bar and worked with the crew. Peggy's hair fell over her face in wisps which she brushed back in futile motions between plunges of the planting bar and setting of the seedlings. It wasn't strength so much as a quality of drive — of will and single-minded purpose — that she exuded.

The very qualities that made her an extraordinary supervisor and executive when she was a young woman in her twenties were apparent here. Her quiet example and thrust sparked the men better than any exhortation from me could have done. By midafternoon the planting quality improved and everyone was setting to with gusto, but we still wouldn't get done by day's end.

I hiked over to where the machine-planting was coming to an end. The machine-planters were doing stub runs — planting the short rows across the ends. There was much pumping-up of the mechanism and turn-around maneuvering during the short runs. They smiled. I knew the satisfaction of completing a seeding.

"We could use some more trees to plant the stub end of the old planting," Paul said. "We never did that and while we're here . . ."

I brought over a bundle from the hand-planters. As I left I heard debate about who would drive the tractor and who would plant.

The machine-planting was finished by late afternoon; by nightfall we had only 2,000 trees left for hand-planting. I paid the crew. We'd plant the remainder on the morrow — just the family.

Best day of all. Weather same as yesterday, and morning started with a pair of loons flying over the little lake, splashing down for landing after much calling and crying. Good omen, loons. But that's silly; can't think of an animal or growing thing that isn't a good omen. It's just I'm fond of loons, and when I'm away from the land I miss their call.

We gathered around the remaining bundles after breakfast, leaning on our planting bars. We could have gone into the cutover area; there were some patches left to go. But I felt like spot-planting the earlier plantations, where there were open swaths. "I'll go between the two creeks. Always meant to do that and never have."

"I'll go on the hill over there," Paul said. "That's bothered me, that open space. We had tractor trouble and missed it a few years ago." And so we each went to our own place and put in the trees in privacy and with some leisure, taking a little extra care in the planting and for once not feeling that there was so much to be done we couldn't take the time to dally. Somehow, suddenly, there were no seedlings left and we gathered up the bars with regret. Off somewhere an American bittern was pumping — "swamp pump," the folks call them.

We held the family Memorial Day picnic under the big white pine atop the ridge, where we could see both lakes. We were all together — all five sons, grandchildren, wives — and the campfire smoke wafted by each of us, driven by a changeling wind. Then came the smells of pancakes and warming blueberry sauce and of sausage. The weather was damp and overcast at first, like yesterday's, but it warmed and the sun broke through as I took all the younger children to inspect the beaver dam at the outlet of the second lake. But someone had come during late winter and had trapped the animals out; no new ones had moved in yet. I wish we could stop the trapping — there are few beavers left.

We went to the township cemetery and gathered around Dad's grave. He'd asked to be buried there, in the place overlooking the river, a granite boulder from the fields marking his grave. It is flanked by two spruce — trees he liked nearly as much as the tamaracks. My sons and I had buried him as he had wished, without undertaker or folderol; just a family giving honor to its own with love, simplicity, and our own hands. Now we stood in a circle holding hands as we had that day eight years before. I wanted to say something now about him and his life, but Smith said, "He was a good man." There was nothing else to say and we went home, back to the farm.

Then it began to rain — a good, strong, steady downpour that will settle the seedlings into the ground.

5

A Matter of Turf

DEER HUNTING FOR THREE DAYS now, red-clad hunters converging on all easily accessible patches of
woods. The neighbors and I have posted our lands, seeking to discourage heedless, often careless invaders, and
to give livestock and children a better chance for survival. The children are kept close and compelled to wear
red clothing, so as to lessen the likelihood of being
mistaken for a deer (though we all know that in poor
morning or evening light color distinctions disappear
and there is heightened risk of a hunter shooting at any
moving shape — it's happened).

Tomorrow is a weekday and most city folk will have
departed. I mark the calendar and make preparation
for my annual Day of Devotion; I have never told anyone I call it that, though the family knows I go on a
day-long retreat in the woods. I lay out the clothes,
including thermal underwear, make sandwiches, set

out thermoses for soup and for coffee, and fill the jacket pocket with raisins. Compass, whistle, knife, rope, and extra gloves are in the kangaroo pouch of the jacket, where they are always kept, just as ski goggles never leave the pocket of my ski jacket. It's a precaution learned over years of experience with marauding children who forget to return what they borrow. The weather promises to be in the twenties, possible light snow; there are residual patches among the trees. I set the alarm for 5:30; daylight is at 7:25.

I started the annual retreat practice accidentally nine years ago, as an antidote to the disrespectful intrusion on nature that hunting season brings, and in response to my resentment of the intruders. Not that I dislike people coming on the land. I've often found strangers and tourists stopping to look at the plantation, and sometimes getting out of their cars; and I've gone over to befriend them and to explain anything they wished to know about growing trees. I have at times made good friends that way, like the curious Australian couple who stopped and asked so many questions several years ago. I'd taken them for a walk through the plantation, and then through the wilder parts and through the marsh to the river, where we watched muskrats, kingfishers, and finally, an osprey diving for fish. They'd stayed for the day, then camped overnight. Another day, and another, for nearly two weeks; we spent evenings learning about the Australian outback and the coral reef, about their lives. He had fought in the Second World War in Burma — a young officer in the British army who settled in Australia after the war.

Only by chance, and long after they had left, did I learn that he was a larger-than-life war hero — decorated, written about, known and notable to many — and later a pioneer in developing business enterprises in various parts of Australia, particularly the remote and exotic areas. To me, at the time of our meeting, he was a short stocky man of insatiable curiosity, on a long camping tour of the United States; and she a reserved, sensitive person, petite and auburn-haired, whose upbringing and manner disguised warmth, a keen mind, and penetrating judgment. We have corresponded since, and the encounter has become for me a touchstone with what is good in life. There have been others. The farm and its lifeway are a bridge to many meaningful, shared human relationships within the family and outside of it. Yet some intrusions are resented: the man who traps beavers and leaves none; the hunters who shoot anything that moves (like the fox vixen last year).

I anticipate the morrow. It is getting late and my advice to the children holds for me as well: hurry to bed and to sleep so the morrow will come sooner. My wife is still reading, and I stroke her hair. "It should be overcast tomorrow but not too cold," she says, acknowledging my plans.

No two of these Days are alike, though they begin with the same clothes and the same quiet coffee making in the sleeping household. Once outside the differences begin. Today there are no crystalline stars; no pale, dipping moon; no sparkle in the snow. It is just plain dark, a soft humidity to the air. The frozen grass of last summer is brittle underfoot, and the few patches of crusted snow are to be avoided for their noise. At first it feels cold and clammy, but the exertion of walking in my bulky sheathes of clothes warms me to the point of opening my collar; soon I'd be very cold.

The walk is nearly a mile, following the roundabout winding path first through the plantation, then the natural tree stand; through tag alder, marsh, and finally to the top of a little knoll near the river, to the misshapen jack pine my sons refer to disrespectfully as "Dad's sitting tree." It is *not* a sitting tree, though I do sit in it. It is a blind where I can share the life around me unobserved and unintrusive; a station in space where I can partake of creation; a window on the world — no, not a window, because as the day goes on, through cold, damp, solitude, and ultimately through knowledge of the life around me, I have become part of it, and not an onlooker as "window" would imply.

It is still dark, there is as yet no hint of daybreak — which is good and as intended. I will sit in this tree throughout the day — until night falls and utter dark returns again — without moving. But it is *not* a sitting tree. The family knows this, but cannot resist teasing me for my foibles.

I come to the tree breathless and overheated, but not having made undue noise. I should wait to cool off, but I am anxious and climb up the gnarled branches ten feet to the fork where a small plank has been wedged for a seat, leaving my legs free to dangle. I hang the rifle on a branch stub, and push the coffee thermos into a crevice. I make ready for the cold — which will probably be unbroken unless the sun comes out at midday — and begin to listen.

The woods are still silent, most animals asleep or cowed by the noise of my passage (though I doubt most humans would have heard). It usually takes fifteen to twenty minutes after a human's footsteps have ceased or his scent has disappeared for animals to begin to move about again; I've noted this often from this perch as stray hunters came through or after my own arrivals. And strangely, none of the hunters have ever noticed me in the tree; nor do most animals look up — only those who fear owls, hawks, or eagles. Fox and deer look about them and scent the air in all directions, but they do not look up.

As graying dawn begins to seep into the dark of night it is plain that this will not be a spectacular sunrise: no bright carmine clouds, no golden-hued mist floating over the low places; just a softening of the darkness, a gradual illumination, imperceptible to the human eye as the slow, patient hands of the universe turn the rheostat slowly and steadily.

I muse about the immensity of the universe, the earth spinning, and me — one of billions — sitting in a jack pine . . . when an explosion of sound a few feet away startles me. It is probably only a fraction of a second before I recognize the sound, but it seems my

fright lasts several seconds, and my heartbeat is much faster. It has come from underbrush nearby; I can hear small, frozen branches snap as the clumsy wingbeats blunder through. The partridge flies clear, is airborne and visible. Similar abrupt awakenings sound nearby now, and a total of five birds rise and fly. Had they suddenly awakened? Been spooked by a predator? No other signs or sounds. They are usually the first to awaken, and more than once have taken me off guard.

No birdcalls yet.

In the distance a door slams. Sounds carry for about two miles to the human ear, probably farther to some animals' ears. I've found little animal reaction to these distant sounds in the past; the animals seem to differentiate between them and closer, more threatening sounds.

Birds now. Light fluttering of chickadee wings as the birds seek pine seeds in the cones; their gray, white, and black markings are distinct in the increasing light. Nuthatches, the black-capped kind. All around now vague shapes become clearer: a clump of hazel brush, no longer a mass of black; individual jack pine, aspen, and willow, no longer a forest's silhouette. A trail I had walked not quite an hour before; faint marks of feet visible in the pattern of the supine marsh grass. Trees, shrubs, and landmarks in the distance still indistinct.

A movement catches my eye, almost directly in front of me, where the patridge had risen. A bedraggled fox moving out at a sedate trot, slowing to sniff the trail I had made, pausing directly below me to look about. It had made no noise in coming through the brush, at least none I could hear. Apparently the fox has not caught any patridge this morning, because it resumes trotting through the little clearing about the knoll, probing for scent of mice. The fur matted, the flanks thin, ribs are showing. This is not an arrogant, well-fed specimen, just a hungry, foraging forest animal whose living is becoming skimpier with the advance of late autumn into winter.

Ernest Thompson Seton has done well with his treatment of foxes, both in prose and in his pen-and-ink drawings. Perhaps his anthropomorphism is not as offensive as that of some other writers because Seton spent much time in careful observance and was a naturalist at heart. Note to myself: reread Seton this winter (I've been collecting his first editions and ought to enjoy them more often).

The fox is still probing, crisscrossing the clearing, patrolling its edges. It has been doing this for nearly twenty minutes; would it react to bird sounds? Squirrels?

Evening grosbeaks flock in, bright colors emphasizing that it is daytime and that other parts of the globe have now coasted into darkness. Yellow, black, and white, they chip and chirrup as finches do — social and gregarious birds. It reminds me that I'd watched cedar waxwings sitting on a pin-cherry branch not far from this spot in summer, passing a berry from one bird to the next, back and forth among four of them, until one finally ate it. The grosbeaks are exploring seedpods among the dried-out milkweed stalks — some noisily in the grass, others hanging on precariously to the stalks. The fox does not seem to mind. I have never seen pine grosbeaks here — perhaps the trees are not tall enough; they are slightly larger birds, as raspberry red as their cousins are bright yellow-white-black.

Squirrels start up: first one chattering in the distance, then another about forty feet away but out of sight. When deer hunting, I frequently curse the noisy squirrels for giving away my movements, though I'm sure the deer have no need of such warnings — my own clumsy human sounds and scents would be enough to alert any self-respecting deer. The fox's ears react to the squirrel sounds, but the fox keeps foraging, nosing the grass as it moves.

I cough very lightly, covering my mouth to cloak the source, and the fox vanishes after freezing for a moment — a pause of a second or two — leaving behind a faint whisking sound of grass, like the aftertaste of good wine, and then the silence and the memory.

Getting a cup of coffee requires time. It has to be done slowly and carefully, with stiff and numb hands. With the activity below me, I have not been aware of growing cold but it is obvious that I have become clumsy. The coffee smells good, as I enjoy the warmth of the cup seeping through the gloves.

There is again the sound of a distant door slamming — probably the youngsters heading down the driveway for the quarter-mile hike to the country road where the school bus stops. A few minutes later: the distant rumble of the bus, its peculiar motor noise the only one of its kind. Nearer; then clanking gears, door opening and shutting, more gears and a resumption of rumbling. The bus sound is all so clear here, a mile away, although totally indiscernible inside the house. What other sounds are commonplace to the animals that I don't even hear? Old Mr. Hansen chopping wood two miles away? Cars on the road? The milk truck passing by on its rounds to the few remaining dairy farms? The mailman on his midday round, opening and slamming mailbox doors, starting and stopping his ancient car? There are only three families in nearly two square miles; yet how much noise we create —

and it is selectively treated by the animals around us.

Chuck-chuck-chuck of a pileated woodpecker. I've seen signs of their workings throughout the year, but we have not met. Now it flies nearly overhead, from a tree on the neighboring knoll to a bigger aspen in a clump sixty feet past me. It is as big as a crow — vivid red crest, with white-and-black body markings. Soon there is a resumption of the chunk-chunk of the big beak digging into deadwood to pick out insects; before long there will be another oval hole to tell who has been feeding there.

The woodpecker ranges back and forth in the course of the day: feeding first in the one place, then in the other, giving its chickenlike clucking call; flapping overhead. In the distance I can hear another pileated calling and feeding, but I never see the two together; nor the second at all, for that matter. Separate territories. Would there be conflict if one transgressed? I doubt it, having seen two feeding in the same general area at other times. Perhaps it is just a matter of convenience, this territorial arrangement. Yet I must admit there is much I don't know about the behavior or ways of these birds, or about anything else. Just a little about a lot of things.

Both birds feed separately all day, and the one within my view appears oblivious to me. At times he is near enough to observe, clutching the tree with sharp, long claws — the stubby tail pried against the trunk, the great tufted head whipping back and forth as chips and splinters fly. Then there are occasional pauses for eating or rest, and a resumption of the pecking. I can discern no cause for the changes from one patch to the other and back.

Rifle shots in the distance. Some hunters, probably local people, are on a drive. One group stands down-wind of the area being driven, the other group beats through the woods toward the standers. It is not my way, though I don't begrudge them theirs.

The cold seeps into my bones, tempting me to climb down and stretch, to move a bit. Why not walk through the tag alders? — make a game of being silent in that brush with its many dead branches, in that skeleton world now that the leaves have been stripped by the season? Even deer make noise moving through it, and few people have the knack of doing it quietly. Duane Dunkley showed me one time; he had learned from his father. Theirs is an Indian family — the men stocky and short, the younger women usually lissome and petite. Duane, heavier than I by a hundred pounds though scarcely taller, took the tag alder swamp at a fast lope, with large strides and twisting movements. The knack was in having an experienced eye that would pick the place to set your feet, choos-ing each stepping place, and using momentum to stride over deadfalls and tangled branches. Over the years I'd gotten skilled enough to circle feeding deer and come stalking from downwind. But my skill was small compared to Duane's; he insisted that his father, now in his sixties, was better still.

The chilliness makes the notion alluring, though I know at the end I will be sweating in my heavy clothes, and there is no point to it; there are no deer in the tag alders this morning or they would be moving, feeding by now, and I would see or hear them. Besides, that kind of hunting belongs to another day. I fish out the soup thermos, tell myself that rubbing hands or chafing feet brings only modest warmth, and drink soup instead.

Suddenly there is an unusual visitor, a sharp-shinned hawk come out of nowhere, it seems, flying straight at my tree and me. It happens so fast I do not even set the cup aside: there he is, coming straight on. Then he veers slightly, passing five feet from me and looking huge at full wingspread, his head turned toward me, our eyes level and locking for an instant; and then he is silently gone. Had I looked an intriguing morsel to him? An oddity to be inspected? Like the animals below me who did not look up, it had not occurred to me to glance upward either. Even as I write my heart beats faster and he looks larger than life to my memory's eye. How must he seem to a mouse, a chipmunk, as he silently appears from nowhere, a sudden shadow preceding the deadly talons by an instant?

I have called owls before, answering their hoots, and one year I even attracted them to the tree. But this visitor was uninvited.

It is nearing noon and I fish out a sandwich, carried nude so to speak and not wrapped in noisy paper. It has collected a few tiny balls of wool from the jacket pocket, a little dirt, but it is a quiet sandwich, and it tastes good. A few crumbs of home-baked bread float toward the ground, passing my morning offering of tobacco sprinkled on the first fork of the tree. It has become silent, even the birds disappear as most creatures seem to do around the middle of the day. Only the squirrels are still at it, and here and there a blue jay squawks. I find it difficult to distinguish between the blue jay's cry of alarm and his familial shrieks.

Then a gunshot nearby, and another. How indescribably loud and alien — how startling. A shock. The sound waves envelop me; this noise could have come from beneath the tree, though actually its source was a quarter of a mile away. Voices. A man's: "You missed him, he ran that way, into the wind. Let him go." And another's, answering: "All right." Neighbors — I recognize the voices.

I hear them a little while, their feet crunching on snow patches and breaking limbs, as they go the other way. Then I hear a deer, coming fairly fast and making its own peculiar racket. They, too, break branches, though it's a finer sound. A man's foot stepping on a dead limb sets off a resonance, while a deer breaks smaller stuff. I reach for the rifle and unlock the safety, for if it was the right kind of deer, medium-sized yearling or doe, I would take my annual quota. It is still coming, when the wire fence that separates my land from the neighbors' squeaks and rattles. It sounds as though someone were climbing over it, then sounds again. Two people? No footsteps, though the deer keeps coming; I would see it soon, following the runway at the foot of the knoll.

Then it is in view — a spike buck of good size, well fed and in prime. I raise the rifle to aim when I see the tiny fawn catch up. The buck must have cleared the fence in an easy leap, but the fawn has tried to run through it, become tangled, and freed itself with difficulty. I have heard accounts of orphaned or strayed fawns attaching themselves to young males, but have never seen it before. Now the two are ambling past; the buck looks over his shoulder once at the coming fawn. I pass up the shot.

Two years ago I watched a grizzled old buck walk out of the woods, his proud rack glinting in the sun. That, too, I passed up. Such an old animal would have stringy and tough meat, and the only excuse for shooting was to possess the rack, which would fall off soon enough of its own accord. Trophies were for others, and I still relish the thought of the proud buck as he slowly grazed across my field of vision. Now I let the spike buck go; once orphaned was enough for the little fawn.

A couple of minutes and they are gone; I hear them for a while even after they leave my view; a squirrel scolds at them from a jack pine clump; then it is quiet once more.

Ducks splashing down in the frost-rimed river a quarter mile to my right. Flap-flap of wings, scudding, and quacking as they feed. The local ducks have been gone for several weeks, and the major migrations from Canada have passed. These are stragglers, making the good life last and stretching their stay; mallards most likely. They don't sound like teal or bluebills.

Geese overhead, a small flight; too high and the light too poor to distinguish the type. Earlier in the autumn, amid the Canadas and the snow geese, there were wild swans. I got up nights two or three times to stand outside and listen to their overflight; in the stillness their calls and occasionally their wingbeats were plain. When the full moon is high on a clear night they can be seen. The sounds of their flight and their calls are haunting, because more than others they connote coming winter, just as five or six months from now they will trumpet returning spring. Their spring sounds are warm and welcome, but the fall flights evoke strong pangs in me — melancholy? A sharp reminder of inexorably passing seasons and time? A call to ready myself for winter in my own way, psychologically and emotionally? Words for the hyperbole elude me, but the sensation of surging excitement is real.

The birds are more active now, feeding once again in the late afternoon. Somehow my mind has registered the sounds of the mailman during the hours passed, the school bus bringing children home, other farmstead noises, but they have all become peripheral. Even the single noises of squirrels and jays, of ducks, geese, and the by-now-ordinary travels, cluckings, and poundings of the pileated woodpeckers have become routine and peripheral. The cold and cramps have become numbnesses and agues; the focus of awareness is elsewhere. Every tree, outcropping, bare spot, and bush has been viewed, examined, and put in place so that as small an event as a nuthatch landing on a limb sixty feet away registers automatically.

The larger aspects have been considered too in the long, cold hours that have melded to make this day: the contours of the land, and how they came to be.

Primeval lake, ice shields, glaciers and their retreat; glacial Lake Agassiz nearly fifty miles to the west, in low terrain. Then warmer times, vegetation, seasons, once perpetual winter had given way. Generation after generation of flora and trees, the organic remains of forebear species giving nourishment to the new; more dominant types crowding out less adaptive ones — scrub oak to aspen to jack pine to spruce to white pine.

I speculate once again on the people who have been before me in this place. Chippewas for the last two hundred years; Sioux before them. Mound builders and Middle Mississippians — their shell-tempered clay potsherds are clear signposts. Copper-culture Indians traveling from Isle Royale to the prairies five thousand years ago; a few knife and spearpoint fragments have been found. Migrants — moving west to east, from Bering Strait inland and southward, as the archeologists and anthropologists say? — or coming from the east, as some Indian legends have it? At any rate, hardy, questing people thirteen thousand years ago and before. A complete skeleton was found and dated over at the Lake Agassiz site, where early travelers had fallen through the ice during their travels. It was a young woman. What had her companions felt? How did the death affect them? Had they perceived a need to ascribe it to supernatural intent or design, or could they deal with disaster and grief on their own terms?

A faint drizzling sleet; it has not warmed above thirty-two degrees all day. I pull the hood over my red beret, careful not to cover my ears and muffle hearing.

Now the little fox will look scragglier yet on his forays, and the birds will go for cover. Dark will come sooner owing to the overcast; the shapes are already becoming indistinct and melding into one another. Is reality the shapeless blob before me, or the individual branches, twigs, and growths I saw in clearer light? The latter, I conclude, my limited human perceptive organs notwithstanding. Sound — in space, on the moon, on a planet — is reality, even if no one is there to receive it: the waves that constitute it are there. And so are the objects and growths and living organisms before me.

Well, who else had come by here? Schoolcraft on his search for the Mississippi's source? Count Beltrami looking for the same but going off on a tangent seven miles northwest of this spot and missing fame and fortune as a result? Vikings, Irish, Phoenicians, Jews, as some would have it? Maybe, maybe not. At any rate, humans for many thousands of years; flora and fauna in waves, progressions, cycles, and cataclysms since this planet came to be. The elements and seasons, the inexorable, the capricious, and the deliberate — birds dropping seeds in their excreta and humans planting seeds and seedlings in the soil. Accidental and intentional. Australian friends and beaver trappers.

This little patch, these few acres open to my view — what a grand and awe-filling thing of which, mortal, I am small part. I have felt my way through it this day. In darkness I climb down slowly from the tree. My limbs are stiff and I squat on the ground, then kneel to restore circulation gradually. The walk home is slow, a transition to the routines, demands, relationships of the world we have chosen to make for ourselves, which exist within a small range of what is available. But it is good to be able to be.

I suffered from psychic leg cramp this morning and decided to stretch my legs. Yesterday's communion was still palpable, the mood of observing, of absorbing still pervasive. I wanted to carry it forward, apply it to a larger, more active arena. Waking early I dressed and fixed lunch hurriedly, left a note for the sleeping family, and emerged into the dark of a north-woods day that promised to be much like the one before.

I hunted Morph Meadows. Elsewhere this patch of world would be called tundra, as in Alaska. Canadians in upper Manitoba call it "bush." It is a huge marsh — its grasses up to six feet high, dotted by islands of higher ground on which aspen, brush, and a few pines tangle and struggle, setting tenuous roots. In the center is a deep little lake upon which one comes suddenly: one step from marsh grass to lake water, which starts abruptly and is deep even at the edge — a precipitous, dangerous dropoff. The grassy lakeshore presents an anomaly in that it is higher than the surrounding marsh, as is the lake level. This oddity is caused by the winter freezing and heaving of the frozen ground, comparable to the effects of permafrost. Yet one cannot perceive the slight rise in ground elevation while approaching, and the few people venturing into the marsh regularly are aware of the presence of the dangerous lake and approach it with cau-

tion. Morph Lake is not the only danger: even greater
is the risk of getting lost. One can wander for hours,
for days, without emerging, and there is little to sustain life; walking in the marsh is difficult in most
places, and next to impossible in the rest.

Wind blows in waves across the supple grass, and
the island shapes in the distance blend and merge with
each other and with the irregular shorelines carved
into peninsulas, outreachings. The grassy marsh bays
reach into the highland, making a pattern of late-
autumn gold, yellow, and brown that the imminent
winter ice and snow will bleach to grayish white by
spring. Then, before greening, it will be a tinderbox,
a fire hazard dreaded by foresters, conservationists, and
fire fighters. Great blazes have roared across portions
of the meadows in years gone by, creating fire storms
and avalanches of roaring flame that engulfed wildlife,
grass, and island growth. These fires were difficult to
extinguish — impossible in the marsh — and fire lines
had to be established on the surrounding higher
ground. There were accounts of fire crews getting lost,
of injuries and hardship, though I don't know if anyone ever perished.

Waterfowl and birds nest in Morph Meadows in
great numbers; migrating flocks descend in the spring.
There is talk of flooding the marsh to diminish the
spring and late fall fire danger and to further enhance
the nesting.

It is many miles across, from one end to the other.
Beyond it to the east is the Third River, feeding Lake
Winnibigoshish. The area of the meadows is over

twenty-seven square miles. There are no roads or trails, save a partial corduroy leading toward, but not as far as, Morph Lake. The road is not usable for cars in wet weather.

Walking in the meadows is exhausting. Feet roll over humps and hummocks, then plunge into ankle-deep water. One hunts the islands, watching for deer crossing the meadow from one island to another. It is a paradise for the hunter who tracks, stalks, still-hunts.

I love this wild, untamable country, and respect its dangers as well as its beauties — its great richness of wildlife and space, of color, wind, and challenge. And I am very conscious of the expanse of the marsh and its hazards — aware that the risk is increased by hunting there alone, and that it would be most difficult to walk out if lost or to wait for help if injured while I work my way to the heart of the meadows.

Of course, I have a compass with flip-up cover and cross hairs to take azimuths and back readings, and I know before I head into high grass to look back for landmarks and trees that stand out. But there are times when my heart pounds a little — when a landmark has vanished into general silhouette as I look back from the meadows, or as one foot sinks and I go knee-deep into icy water: Have I come this close to Morph Lake unwittingly? Stumbled into freezing, pneumonia, exhaustion, drowning? No, only a little pothole.

Today I walked 1½ miles from the car through high ground, letting a peninsula take me out as far as possible before having to brave the marsh. The ground showed much traffic from deer, even a place where dried ferns, more brown and sere than green now, had been trampled by competing bucks. Branches showed where velvet had been rubbed from antlers during ill-tempered days when new horns harden; and the outer bark was brown and shredded, dried tendrils hanging alongside the exposed pale wood. Nearby were tracks from feeding, browsing deer; a few fawn prints. Had they been spectators at the conflict?

I hunted hard all day, but had no luck. I was sweating even in the twenty-degree sunlight, feet soaked from midmorning on; they get cold quickly when you stop walking. I set a steady pace heading back, paying obeisance to the dark waters of Morph Lake on the way; they are almost black, foreboding.

It was a long, hard walk to highland; the sun was low. I had tarried today, absorbing the experience through the filter of yesterday's passive retreat. Eventually I hit high ground, and relished the easier walking among trees, brush, ferns, when again land ended and I faced more meadow — seemingly endless marsh!

I'd strayed off course! Hitting an island, not mainland! But there were no islands anywhere near the peninsula I had used to enter! Where was my point of entry? My car? How much daylight was left? Anyone else around? I hadn't seen anyone all day.

Last year a hunter strayed and became lost south of Winnibigoshish, in easier country than this, and while trying to walk out he panicked, ultimately drowning in shallow waters while striking out toward a far-off light from a cabin. I know foresters and rangers who have been lost in Morph Meadows, but found late at night

by other members of their crews as a lucky result of
warnings to never to go in here alone. But I had no
crew, no companions this day! And only a pocketful of
raisins and a candy bar! Did I have matches? Yes — I
patted the pocket, fingering them with reassurance,
my heart pounding, my spirits frenzied.

There was the beginning of true panic now: the im-
pulse to run, shout and yell, lash out in some way. I
wouldn't starve, I told myself; I could make a fire,
build a lean-to. But I had been stranded once in
weather like this, and knew the exhaustion that comes
from being cold and tired, the acceleration of fatigue from being wet. And now the even faster deterio-
ration caused by fear. I struggled for calmness, for
clearness of thought; I could not have strayed far, because I'd taken bearings, oriented by Morph Lake and
the waning sun. Make use of the remaining daylight,
I told myself. Breathe slowly, deeply, then walk around
slowly, calmly, and reason it out.

I crisscrossed the island, looking for sense of orientation and place, for framework of reference to guide me
out. I knew there were no islands anywhere near the
peninsula I had taken in that morning, nor in or near
that end of the meadows, so where was I? Back and
forth across the island, meadows at each side; resur-
gence of panic. Then, instead of the pointless and fearful crisscrossing, I traversed at right angles: back to
the meadows again! The other way: indistinguishable
woods, brush, ferns, like the rest of the island. Then
sudden recognition: I was back at the trampled ferns
of the mating place. I *had* come back to my point of

entry, from a slightly different angle, and had simply crossed the narrow thumb of the peninsula, mistaking it for an island!

I was relieved to be plodding back to my car at dusk, enjoying the regular stride and pace; the heartbeat was slowly subsiding; my spirits were comforted by the sense of rescue, of being saved. From what? My own stupidity. No, not stupidity: a confusion, loss of orientation and judgment. How secure was my tree perch of yesterday, my safe and secure haven of status quo as against the uncertainties of striking out. I am chagrined at having been confused and panic-prone.

Sobering thought: Is this what insanity feels like — a terrifying amalgam of confusion and fear, of not knowing where one is nor how to escape from I know not what?

I knew where I was going, and how to get there. Even when "lost" I'd known where I was in relationship to the central Morph Lake, and could always have gone back there after an uncomfortable night and begun again. So I hadn't been utterly lost — I had been in no danger of imminent death. And yet, consider my fright and unreasonable fears. How had early nomads felt? The first wanderers into this then-unknown country many thousands of years ago? Had they felt fear, panic, confusion at times? Dreaded unknowns? Monsters? Spirits? How much fear was in the lives of earlier man?

At home I am warm, fed, clean, and comfortable. The weather report says there will be a cold snap tonight — far below zero. I'm glad I made it in tonight.

It was a different kind of a retreat today, not only as a result of being lost. It was a day spent in spaciousness contrasted to yesterday's confining mode, a day spent in activity and movement. I was a miniscule particle, an erratically moving atom, subject to forces far beyond my knowing and control, unlike yesterday's all-seeing, all-knowing observer and sharer. Microcosm, macrocosm; one day, the next. And yes, even the fright of being lost included, it was good and it rounded out the retreat, because it brought home to me once again the danger of hubris, of thinking I know it all, can manage it all.

Before my mind's eye tonight there are seas of meadow grass undulating in the wind, supple and sensuous, and the mental image is mixed with the forms of yesterday's unwavering trees. Tomorrow both will be covered with snow.

6

Dog Pack

IT HAPPENED DURING our third winter on the tree farm, when the three older boys were still at home, still in high school, and before the two younger ones were born. It was a cold night — fifteen below — and the stars were glistening; the white of the snow was iridescent in the clear air. The young dog woke me with his whimpering, and I looked at the clock, noting it was a few minutes past 5 A.M. The old dog slept on, wheezing, and the puppy whimpered again.

It was not an intruder, and not a fire that aroused him; nor did he have needs of his own, or he would have barked or yipped. I got up and looked out the upstairs bedroom window, and saw nothing amiss. The path to the driveway had been shoveled out of the two-foot-high snow. It was empty, and so were the driveway and the yard. I had about decided to go back to bed and sleep the remaining two hours when he whimpered again. He was a good dog, and had something to say. I padded downstairs in the dark. The dog nosed the door, but caution made me slip on my boots, heavy coat, and hat, and reach for the .22 rifle hanging by the door. I would never keep a loaded or exposed firearm about a house with young children, but the boys were old enough to have been instructed, and had proved themselves careful. There was never a shell in the chamber, but the rule was that whoever used the rifle had responsibility for fully reloading the fifteen-shot magazine. On a whim, I shoved the young dog and the older one — who had now struggled to wakefulness — into the bathroom and closed the door. I opened the front door quietly and still saw and heard nothing. I reached back, flipped the switch for the yard light, and headed for the barn.

There was a scrambling sound from within, then one shape after another came hurtling through a broken window. I looked in momentary disbelief at the gaping hole, where four panes and woodwork had been broken out, and then I recognized the forms: dogs — floundering, scampering, struggling through the snow. The sheep! They'd been after the sheep!

I aimed at the retreating shapes in the snow and fired at one after another. On the sixth trigger-pull the gun was empty. I had counted twelve dogs, none of which I recognized in the murk as belonging to neighbors.

When I returned to the house the lights were on and everyone was up. "Dogs. A pack. They got in the barn."

"Did they get my sheep?" Smith had been raising

prize-winning sheep for 4-H, and the registered ewe and two yearlings belonged to him.

"Haven't looked yet. Where are the shells?"

"There aren't any more," one of the boys said. "We used them up the other day."

"And didn't tell me? And didn't replace them? Get dressed, Smith, and get the flashlight. I'll meet you at the barn." I uncased the deer rifle, loaded it, pocketed extra shells, and went out again. The dogs had fled; if I had hit any with the .22, they would be out of sight in the snow and I'd have to track, using the light. Smith met me at the barn and we went in.

"Sorry about the shells and the gun not being loaded," he said, and we walked into the only occupied corner of the barn, the sheep pen. (The hog pen was used only from April to November, when we bought young pigs and fed them until butchering time; and we had not yet begun with feeder cattle that year.)

The ewe was still alive, but her belly had been ripped open and her entrails dragged out. She was bleating and helpless, lying on her side and kicking feebly. The young sheep were dead.

Smith had tears in his eyes and was close to hysteria. "Shoot her, Dad. Shoot her, don't let her suffer. Oh, those sons of bitches." He had raised her from a lamb and had won a blue ribbon showing her at the county fair. She had been bred, and we had helped when the lambs were born. Her udders had been plugged and I had had to show Smith how to strip the teats until the first milk began. Then the newborn lambs — more black than white, as Hampshires tend to be (though they would turn white later) — had to be started on the teat. "It's drinking, it's drinking," Smith had shouted, and the whole family had stood around watching the miracle of the wobbly lambs drinking their first mother's milk, butting the udder while still unsteady on their legs. I don't think I'd ever seen my oldest son so happy or joyous. He had gone on to win further prizes both with the ewe and with her lambs. Now the lambs were dead and I had to shoot the ewe. They had all been too badly torn by the dogs for any meat to be salvaged, though it appeared the dogs had not eaten.

Since the .22 was empty and the deer rifle was too powerful for what I had to do, I rummaged in the house until I located a handgun I kept, loaded it, and returned to the barn to complete the disagreeable task. The ewe was still on her side; she had not moved. She bleated faintly and tried to rise, feebly moving her forelegs. The hind legs had been hamstrung by the dogs, the tendons torn; and the pulsating entrails were visible on the barn floor. I aimed for the central spot on the forehead, the spot at which a properly angled shot produced instant death. It was the method we preferred at butchering time, though I have never been completely easy about killing, whether for food or for self-protection. The thought flashed through my mind that the shot, improperly angled, would only prolong her agony. I had seen this happen at butchering once, some years before, when the bullet had glanced off the slanted forehead bone of a hog, and the animal had run squealing through the pen. But I was procrastinating, putting off that which I disliked doing. I aimed, pulled the trigger; and before the sound of the shot had stopped vibrating in the barn or in my inner ear, she had stopped moving. She died instantaneously, mercifully, and I unloaded the gun and pocketed it, having no further feelings about the necessary act.

Then I checked the dog tracks, all of which angled from the barn toward the driveway across the snow. I found two dead dogs in the snow, and blood spoor heading down the snow-packed driveway. I returned to the house.

"Got two. Mutts. One had a collar. Blood on the driveway." I dressed hurriedly and set out to track, carrying the deer rifle.

Where the driveway came out on the country road, little blood spots trailed both north and south; there must have been two wounded dogs. Twenty-two-caliber bullets leave small holes, and the drops of blood were several feet apart as I followed the road south, downhill. It was still dark, but the sharp contrast between dark trees and shining white snow made the flashlight unnecessary, except to spot the little blood marks on the road. They had turned pink as they melted the snow, and then had frozen.

Nearly a hundred feet ahead there was a flash of movement behind a snowbank piled up by the snowplow. I stopped to look again, to listen, then moved ahead carefully. Any wounded animal is dangerous, as is a trapped or cornered animal. This animal was both wounded and trapped — because it had nowhere to go but over the hard-packed snow of the road; woods and fields were not traversable.

Then the form emerged from behind the snow pile and came toward me. Not moving away to escape, but walking, then loping toward me. A wolf! No. A large dog. A German shepherd — and a very large one. I dropped the flashlight in my pocket, took the rifle off safety, and aimed. The dog was moving steadily, closing the distance and at fifty feet now. I squeezed the trigger, the animal large in the sights, but the rifle did not fire. It had been in the warm house, had picked up condensation or moisture on being brought outside, and the moisture had frozen, disabling the action. During hunting season I rarely brought the rifle indoors, but instead kept it in the milk house or garage overnight to prevent this from happening.

I broke the action of the rifle, raising the bolt, pulling it back carefully so as not to eject the shell, and ramming it home again sharply, hoping to free the action. The dog was close now, and I aimed and squeezed again. This time there was a roar; the dog was slammed to the road by the bullet's impact. It twitched and was dead. I paced off the distance. Twelve feet, from where I had stood to the dead animal. Eighty-five feet, from where I had stood to the snowpile where he had waited in ambush, coming out to charge me.

It was a large specimen, yellow and black, a full-grown male. Even in its death rictus it exhibited a snarl, exposing teeth and fangs. There was a training collar, a choke-type chain, but no trace of leash and no tags. In the country, and even in our nearby villages and towns, there is no licensing requirement, though most people have their pets vaccinated for rabies, and some take the trouble to fasten the rabies-shot tags to the dog collars. Not to this one. I dragged the carcass to the driveway entrance, guessing the weight to be seventy-five or eighty pounds. Then I turned north.

I knew what I would find before I got there, and didn't want to go on. But it had to be done. There was the sound of a shot from the next farm and I walked on, not bothering to track carefully any longer, only occasionally flicking on the light. The blood track was still there, and turned in at the next farm, three-quarters of a mile from mine. It was being operated on shares by a new family; they were friendly people with many children, and very poor. The farmer met me in front of his house.

"I heard the shooting. Dogs?" he asked.

"A pack. They got our sheep."

"D'you get any of them?"

"Three now. A big shepherd — I think he led the pack."

"My dog's been running for days now, kept getting away. You must've winged him, 'cause he came home a little while ago bleeding. Just shot 'im."

"Yeah. I tracked blood."

He shifted uncomfortably. "Sure sorry about your sheep. I don't know what we can do."

"No need to do anything. You know where any of

those other dogs came from or whom they belong to?"

"Haven't seen much of them. I think there's a little one belongs to the resort on the lake, the one three miles down the road. Most of the rest are from town." Town is eleven miles away.

He repeated his apology and offered to stand good for the damages.

"Well," I said. "Maybe you could let me use your Rototiller this spring when you're not in need of it. I haven't got one, and that garden of mine is a back-breaker." We agreed on it, and it was comfortable for both of us.

"Your kids are going to miss that pooch," I said.

"So they will, but a running dog's a menace."

We parted and I walked home. Then I drove to the farm the other side of us, where there was a large dairy herd, to give warning. I found my neighbor in the milking parlor, well into the morning's chores.

"Thought I'd better warn you. We had a dog pack break into the barn and kill the sheep this morning."

"Well, I'll be darned. Mine wasn't in it, was she?"

"No, not so far's I know."

"We kept her in the house last night; always do when it's cold."

"Just wanted to let you know, in case any of the calves are out."

"Well, thanks. You know, we have a rule around here: if anybody sees a stray dog on their place, they shoot it. Even if you know who it belongs to. That goes for mine, too. If they can't stay around the place, they're no good to me."

"Didn't know that. Same goes for mine, if they start running."

He stopped working for a few moments, leaving the milking machine pumping away. "All it takes is for a bunch of them to get together and find a leader," he said, "and the nicest pooches in the world turn into a vicious pack. You wouldn't know they're the same animals."

"Some of these may have come from town," I said.

"I wouldn't be surprised. Of course their owners would never believe it, nor admit it if they did. They'd be liable for the sheep."

"You know, they didn't eat any of the meat. They just tore those lambs, and they got the ewe's belly, from the udder up to the rib cage, and opened her up."

"That's the way wolves do. Except wolves kill to eat. A dog pack will kill just for bloodlust."

He said he'd call the other farmers nearby to give warning to be on the lookout, though we both speculated that with the leader gone, the pack would disappear, the members dispersing to their warm, comfortable homes, the Jekyll-Hyde transformation reversed.

"Too bad about the sheep. I bet those boys of yours are really sick about that."

I nodded, thanked him, and left. Only one more stop, then I'd have to get home and dress for work. (I was teaching school that year.)

The resort people didn't know anything about a dog pack, and weren't willing to talk. Oh, their own pooch had been inside all night; oh no, he never ran. But as I turned to go I heard the dog whimper underneath the porch where he had a sleeping place, and I had my own thoughts about where he had been, but no proof and no means of doing anything about it.

We ate breakfast in silence and then went our ways: Smith, Paul, and Derek to catch the Bemidji school bus; my wife to town, where she was taking college courses; and I to teach eleventh- and twelfth-graders at Cass Lake. I gave Smith a hug as we all left, but he was withdrawn and still hurt.

By evening I had hauled away the sheep, having dragged them far off into the plantation, where birds and animals would dispose of the remains quickly, and in a utilitarian way. Dinner was again a silent meal; no one had much to say. The Labrador, ordinarily an inveterate moocher, somehow sensed the depression and the strained atmosphere and stayed on her rug — near enough to the table to hear any invitations, should they be extended, but wary enough not to ask for handouts. The puppy, whom I had praised that morning for giving the alarm, had no compunctions about begging from the boys. I wasn't supposed to know, but they sneaked food to the dogs from the table. It was a long-standing charade.

"Get away from here, mutt," Derek snapped at the puppy.

"It's not his fault," Paul interceded.

"I bet it was that Toby from the next farm that led

them here," Smith said. It was the first comment he made. "He's been coming here since last fall."

Then we were all talking at once, bursting with pent-up, conflicting emotions, trying to make sense of the senseless event.

"It was so wanton, so useless," my wife said. "Atavistic."

"What's 'atavistic'?" Derek, then in ninth grade, was intellectually curious and probing.

"A throwback, a recurrence of something typical of ancestors," my wife said.

"They acted more like wolves," Smith added.

"But wolves don't act that way," I said. "They'll kill and eat. Few species just kill. No, I don't think it's atavism or a throwback to anything. This was a pack, or a mob, different from instinct or primeval urge."

"D'you remember the wild cat you saw last year, Paul?" I asked. He had spotted a domestic cat that had gone wild, surviving in the woods, as large and fierce as a true wildcat. Cats and dogs were occasionally left abandoned in the woods or strayed there themselves. As a rule they did not survive long; they fell prey to diseases and could not acclimate themselves to the cold, nor hunt effectively over the long haul. But occasionally an animal survived by virtue of its strength, adaptability, and became especially dangerous as a result of its solitary existence.

"I remember," Paul said. "I thought it would jump me from the tree branch it was on. It was during deer hunting. I just stood still and froze, and he finally turned and jumped from one branch to another and disappeared. Big, like a bobcat almost. But these weren't wild dogs, Dad. They were family dogs . . ." The question remained unspoken: could our peaceful, gentle Labradors act in this fashion — become members of a pack, wanton killers?

I have never observed packlike behavior in animals in the wild, nor am I familiar with any reliable accounts. Some species hunt in packs, as wolves and lions, but that is for the purpose of finding food. There is plenty of aggressive behavior other than for food-procuring reasons: for protection against fancied or real attack or threat, when flight is not available; for defense when wounded (even rabbits or deer become vicious then); for demonstrating male dominance during mating contests. These examples and others have been amply recorded, as have the hierarchical and pecking-order dominance struggles — though few animals fighting their own kind will do so to the death, particularly in the higher orders. Behavior such as that of the dog pack in its wanton killing is not a common animal characteristic of wildlife. A concomitance of domestication? Do domesticated animals reflect the pressures, strains, tensions of being "civilized" and crowded as do humans? And do dogs particularly do so, because of their hunting origins and size?

I'd grown up, as had so many of my generation, imbued with the concept of Darwinian evolution, making an unwarranted quantum jump by assuming that human behavior and human nature had also evolved, and had progressed. In later years, particularly since coming to the tree farm, I had gradually changed my view. I had come to view human nature and the human brain as having developed with infinite slowness over the millennia, and as being not very different now from how they were one hundred thousand years ago; I see man as neither a noble savage, come down from Eden to present imperfection, nor as a superior being, having advanced from savagery. Rather, we are a species with substantial brain capacity as well as a little instinctual residue, a species prone — under pressures, tensions, and burden of social ills, and influenced by both opportunity and leadership — to the same sort of packlike conduct as was exhibited by the domesticated dogs in our barn. Wanton destructiveness is a human manifestation that occasionally culminates in genocide, and it is prevalent as a concomitance of "civilization." Prehistoric man may have been fearful and superstitious, but we advanced, modern, civilized humans have become the destructive ones. And our domesticated animals as well? What could I say to my son Paul, and to Smith and Derek, not knowing all the answers myself?

"I've been hunted by a pack. And I've been part of a pack," I said. "I was hunted by a pack when I was a boy in Vienna and had to run for my life when Nazis were pursuing me because I was a Jew."

"Would they have killed you?"

"How did you get away?"

"They would have killed me, yes. Or at least injured

me badly. And I got away by taking risks, darting through traffic, and finally by plunging across the path of an oncoming trolley car. I made it; they had to wait for it to pass. When it had gone, I had disappeared. That's how I got away. Luck and the physical ability that comes from desperation and fear. Others didn't get away. The point isn't that I got away — because if I hadn't you wouldn't be here asking me questions about it — but rather: What made those people turn into a pack?"

"What did?"

"Inner need, opportunity, and their leaders, who urged them on and gave sanction and permission. The need came from the bottled-up anger and frustration of the times, the economy, the history. The opportunity came from the destruction of the social and political system. And the leaders I don't have to tell you about." We talked about it for a while.

"That's why the dog pack killed my sheep?" There was still hurt in Smith's voice.

"You can't draw an exact parallel. After all, dogs are one thing, people another. But yes, I think some of the same essentials were there." And even as I said it, I knew that reading and understanding Freud, Jung, Adler, and Fromm wouldn't take away my son's hurt, nor diminish the seeds of suspicion that were aroused.

"You said you were part of a pack too," Derek pursued.

"Yes. It was during the strike, before we moved here, when there was the riot. Suddenly, in the excitement and the anger of the demonstration it was like a flash point had been reached, and a small group of ten or fifteen out of that crowd of several thousand went berserk. They had a leader, and they went completely out of control, and started beating up people. It was brutal — carnage — and there was no stopping them."

"Were you doing that?"

"No, I recoiled from that. So I guess it wasn't exactly true that I was part of a pack, although I could see how it could happen. And having helped bring about the initial demonstration, and watching it get out of hand, and then being unable to stop the brutality gave me a feeling of responsibility and made me think about what I was doing, and why, and how I was doing it."

"Is that why we moved here?" Paul asked.

"Out of my thinking came a decision I wanted a more wholesome way of living, something farther removed in character and kind from destructiveness and conflict. It had a whole lot to do with our coming here."

"And now we've come here and a dog pack kills the sheep." Smith wasn't about to let up.

"Sure. It's happened. And we plant fifteen hundred willows and they die, and we plant another fifteen hundred and they die too. And the fire wiped out Oberberg's tree plantation and scorched the pioneer cemetery, and his dreams are as dead as the people buried there. And the old logger went out on the coldest night of the year without proper clothes and froze to death (and I still say that was suicide). And whole

peoples and races are killed, and individuals and groups are persecuted and suppressed. And our environment is being maltreated. There is destructiveness — and some of it is random and meaningless, and some of it can be prevented. I feel bad the sheep were killed, Smith. It isn't just your attachment to them, but also knowing you can't do it over, that you've lost nearly three years' time."

"What's the sense of it?"

"That you realize there is destructiveness in life. And being aware of it, that you shape your life and your conduct so as to be constructive. A builder, a planter, a lover of life, however you choose to live it. It doesn't matter so much whether you start with sheep again, or do something else. So long as you do it."

I felt dissatisfied with my explanation. I'd failed to clarify the role of human character; not all humans are capable of destructive behavior. Most are not. The watershed is the contour of an individual's character.

This can't be applied to animals, wild or domestic; and yet the puzzling behavior of dogs in packs remains to be understood. (Perhaps I can suggest to the boys that they read Fromm on the nature of human destructiveness; it's difficult reading.) But one cannot speak of "character" in domesticated animals. Some pet owners would have it that way no doubt, yet it seems inappropriate to me. It's a controversy well enough left alone for this day; there's been enough hurt.

It was a night when everyone went about their own

thing. My wife read, Derek studied, Paul was at his stamp collection, Smith disappeared. I got dressed and put on the snowshoes. I dragged the carcass of the leader dog from the bed of the pickup truck; my efforts to identify it or its owners had been fruitless. I tied a rope to it, and dragged it over the snow through the plantation.

The night was as clear and cold as the one before, the stars bright, the snow lighting my way. I was puffing, perspiring, but kept a steady pace. Plod-plod, a squeak from the binding of the right snowshoe; a faint whispered crunching as the webbing settled in the snow — one foot, the other foot. The surface of the snow was largely unbroken; only occasionally did a solitary branch poke through the crust, for the plantation was young then. Not far from where I had left the sheep, where fox and other kinds of trails crossed the field, I unhitched the rope. The dog's muzzle had remained unchanged — lips peeled back, teeth bared in a snarl.

I turned homeward, the silhouette of the farmstead shaped by the outline of the house and barn and by the big pines in the yard. A couple of yellow-lighted windowpanes could be made out through the lower branches of the trees around the house.

We weep not so much for the dead, as for ourselves — our loss, our fear, our disappointment, our loneliness, our regrets. And part of my answer to destruction was underfoot in the form of the snow-covered seedlings, and part of my answer was in the lighted house.

I trudged home and was confident that Smith would find constructive answers to destructiveness and loss, and that the other boys would too. The thick-frozen ice boomed from the lake — for even the ice contracts, rumbles, grates, and explodes, caught in its own dynamics — and I imagined an echo in the empty barn.

7

Culling

BOB FURMAN, THE YOUNG state forester, came over this morning to help select and mark trees — the first step in culling the natural stands. The big white pines I thought ready to harvest are still growing at a healthy rate and we'll take another look at them in five or ten years. They are fighting off the blister rust, the color at the top is still good, and the waist-level borings we made extracted cross sections of rings showing steady growth. So much for harvesting sawlogs to sell this year and holding out some boards for the house.

Instead, the big spruce on the back hill have to come down (with the exception of four). There is a fatal flaw in each: lightning streaks admitting insect pests and causing rot at the core; old fire scars with the same results. The trees are about 125 years old; I've sheltered under them when caught in the woods by rain. A cluster of five had a little hollow in their midst, covered by an umbrella of branches. The deer like to sleep there, and in the wintertime it's a regular resting place for me when snowshoeing.

Bob senses my feelings and asks if he should mark the trees. "I'll do it," I tell him, and blaze the doomed trees.

As we walk through the brush and interspersed slashing of earlier harvests of aspen and jack pine with the children tagging along, Bob points to the hundreds of spruce seedlings coming up: "The slashings are good shelter. The additional sunlight coming in when the big spruce come out will speed the growth." True, and he is trying to make me feel better.

"As a rule, the spruce on the lower ground and in thin soil won't last long," he goes on. "This type of spruce usually goes a hundred and fifty years to maturity, but the soil is thin, and when you get lower ground eighty-five years is about it. Then the wind and other factors pile up and the time comes to take them out. These have done remarkably well."

It is a hot walk in unseasonable, ninety-degree humid air. Mosquitoes and deerflies are persistent. The children drop out early and leave us, attracted by wild raspberries. It's a good raspberry year. Each year seems to feature a bumper crop of a different kind. Last year it was pin cherries; ground cherries the year before. We put the plantation on the big upland field; after that the ground cherries disappeared. (Reminder: look for fringed gentian. They surprised me last year;

are they to bloom again this year? Where had they come from so suddenly?) My thoughts return to the problem of insects. Bob says I should expect colonies of carpenter ants when we cut the spruce, but to let him know if there turn out to be anything else. He's worried about a sawfly infestation.

We finish selection and marking about noon. Over forty trees, all big. Eight white pine being killed by blister rust, the rest spruce. Drenched by sweat, surrounded by the ever-present biting insects, we ride back to the house and freshen up with iced tea. Bob brought his lunch: homemade bread and wild cranberry jam.

We talk about the advisability of planting cedar in the lowland. "Should be all right providing the sod competition isn't too much, and if it's dry enough. They flood out like any other tree."

"I planted a few jack pines there seven years ago to experiment. They're doing well."

"Then the cedar should do. Jack pine are more susceptible to drowning than cedar."

We dig test holes with an auger to examine soil composition and water content, and agree it's worth a try. So: cedar planting in a year or two.

I like Bob. He is involved in his work and believes in it. We have common ground also in that each of us is consciously trying to establish a particular mode and character of living. And both of us are at home in the north country.

Bob works for State Forestry, helping individuals,

such as myself and the paper-company tree farms, but primarily he is concerned with state forest lands and parks. Young, college-trained people like Bob are resented by some of the older staff whom they supervise. The longtime men learned by doing — logging, fire fighting, planting — and they know a lot. Yet they tend to scoff at planning, at experimentation and innovation. And surely they resent being bossed by a young college man. Bob has never talked about it, but the feelings and relationships are there.

For all his knowledge, academic and applied, he is practical. He too has done his apprenticeship in logging, fire fighting, planting; and he had to depend on such work to support himself during college and to raise his young family. But he has gone beyond.

He leaves after lunch to meet a work crew at the adjacent state park, a small, wild place on a bluff overlooking the river.

I called at Leroy Kersten's to arrange for logging. He had cut and hauled the aspen and jack pine other times.

At his driveway entrance just outside Bemidji his youngest daughter, Kim, long blond hair streaming, comes charging out astride her sorrel horse. A common enough sight in their household, but then I look again and almost drive into the ditch. Kim is not the only rider: the saddle is shared by her mischievous billy goat. Kim is training horse and goat to replicate a stunt she had seen in a magazine photo.

"That's nothing," Leroy laughs. "She's going to make a pyramid on that horse. Goat, dog, cat, rooster. Give her time, she'll get them trained."

No doubt, but hopefully not next to the highway.

Leroy's big Caterpillar is parked on the bed of the big truck; the jammer apparatus for lifting and stacking logs is partially dismembered. Leroy hauls the Cat on this truck, unloads it at the cutting site or nearby, then uses the truck to haul logs. A rubber-wheeled skidding wagon is pulled behind the truck. During operations the skid is pulled by the Cat.

"Finally finished the cutting job for the county," Leroy says. "Got to replace a hydraulic cylinder on the jammer. Had to wait six weeks for the parts."

We inspect the work and drink coffee. Leroy is not much taller than my 5½ feet, but his strength is incredible. I'm no weakling, and can carry a couple of hundred pounds deadweight, but I can't budge the steel skid. Yet Leroy will lift the hitching bar that I could not move more than a few inches and hook the skid to the Cat. Or lift logs, toppling them end over end or pitching them near the skid when we're cutting, when I could barely roll them.

"Oh, I'm used to it, that's all," he would grin. Only we both knew I worked daily with my hands and was fit, and I still couldn't do it.

To top it off, Leroy was badly wounded in the Korean War, major portions of one shoulder shattered by shrapnel, his shoulder and arm operated on and reconstructed surgically time and time again. Once, one side of his face was smashed by a branch broken by a freak wind; the branch hurtled several hundred feet to prostrate the passing man. He recovered, returned to the woods and the work he loves, though he needn't have: by brains and ability he could operate a larger concern and supervise loggers, or go into any one of several other activities. But he doesn't want to, despite the urging of his wife (who's successful at her own business).

The only one-upmanship I can ever muster is my superior skill as a carpenter. At least Leroy's wife thinks so, and makes pointed suggestions to him when they visit us. I suspect Leroy's as good as I am, and just not all that interested. The siding on his house, or the new basement floors or children's rooms are all as neat and as well made as any of my work, even though they resulted from a campaign of several years on the part of Leroy's family to get him to do them.

We talked about the culling. By Leroy's standards it isn't a "real" job, such as he would contract for with others (as he had with me on past occasions, when we had selectively cut aspen and jack pine for pulpwood, saving spruce, Norway and white pine, balsam, tamarack, and birch).

"That's only sixty-five trees," Leroy says. "And they're scattered." He's thinking of the equipment to be hauled in: the skid, pulled by a small Cat, to bring logs from cutting sites to a temporary "yard" central to the cutting, where the truck could load and haul.

"I could do it myself," he says, meaning it would not pay to bring his customary two helpers, but implying also that he was unsure about leaving them unsupervised on a contract job, and about handling all the equipment by himself. "It should take less than a day," he adds — more a question than a statement.

"I'll work with you, and we can go halves," I offer.

"I'll come out and we'll take a look." That means plotting a route through the woods to see whether we could work in two or three arcs from the yard, or whether there would have to be many side trips to cutting sites: time-consuming trips that are hard on equipment and eat up daylight hours.

"We could yard right where we had the first pulp yard last year," I suggest, "and pick up a part load on the way out."

"That'd help." Leroy agrees. "The road's in and I wouldn't have to make another."

He'll be out tomorrow after dinner.

It rained yesterday. Leroy showed up in a ¾-ton heavy-duty pickup, a new acquisition since we'd logged together last year. It was past dinner but we had a beer before setting out in the still-warm evening air.

"You don't want to come," Leroy explains to the pleading Tony and David. "The mosquitoes will pick you up and carry you away. And if they don't, the wood ticks will!"

Wood-tick season ordinarily ends in June. The wet weather has prolonged their cycle this year, and we check hair and bodies carefully each day, especially when we've been in the woods or berrying. The bites aren't dangerous but can result in nasty sores, slow to heal. Besides, Leroy and I have a lot of ground to cover before nightfall.

We drive to the old yard, park, and set out on foot, inspecting locations of the blazed trees. Leroy moves in big, loping strides, over brush and slash, eyeing the blazed trees in relationship to their neighbors, antic‑ipating hang-ups and direction of fall, and above all silently calculating how to bring in Cat and skid.

"I swear you run through the brush to stay ahead of the bugs," I tell him. Keeping up with Leroy is a test of physical fitness. In spring I lose, by midsummer I can almost make it.

Deerflies are in our hair and on our ankles when we stop long enough; mosquitoes are all over. They are a pervasive nuisance. On a Canadian canoe portage years ago I stepped on grassy trail, heavy packs on my back and the canoe on top, when clouds of mosquitoes rose, covering my face — in my nostrils, ears, and my eyes. I had to retreat, tie a kerchief across my face and peer through slitted eyes before setting out on a run. Derek was with me, eleven then, on his first major outing. I covered his face too, told him to run and keep going into the water at the other end. I made two trips, the second time dumping gear into the canoe and shoving off quickly; we lost the pursuers half a mile out on the water. Having known the panic, mosquitoes in lesser numbers no longer frighten me, and like everyone else I have tried every commercial concoction in turn with indifferent results. I notice a bottle of the latest on the dashboard of Leroy's truck.

"Pretty good?"

He shrugs. "Keep forgetting to put it on."

We map out a cutting sequence and pattern that will economize movement of equipment.

"If the damage inside isn't too bad, we can sort sawlogs, bolts, and pulp. Probably get more for bolts than sawlogs even. They've got a special order at the mill, but nine inches minimum at the top."

Ordinarily sawlogs bring the best prices, and constitute the best wood. They are used to produce boards, beams, two-by-fours, and have to be good enough to be sawed to proper thickness and width, and then planed at the sawmill. The longer the sawlog, the better, though sometimes buyers specify desired or minimum lengths. Quite often 100 inches, or a bit over eight feet in length, is the minimum. This is the same length usually required for pulpwood bought by papermills or by manufacturers of composition board and products, where the wood is chipped and then made into composition materials in combination with gluelike substances. Bolts, also running to 100-inch lengths as a rule, can be used for railroad ties, planking, or shoring materials. We don't know why there is the sudden premium on bolts this time, but we are certain the good price will be short-lived. The standard unit of measurement for our kind of cutting is a *double*, meaning two cords, each of which measures eight feet wide by four feet long and four feet high.

The big spruce will all meet the minimum diameter requirement, yielding several 100-inch lengths. The last stick, less than 9 inches in top diameter, will go on the pulpwood pile.

"Bet you hate to see them go," Leroy says as we drive back.

"Better now than windblown this winter," I rationalize.

Leroy comes over after dinner again, off-loading Cat and skid at the yard site, gassing and oiling the battered Cat, checking hydraulic fluid on the jammer mechanism. In the remaining hour of daylight, Leroy proposes to cut a few of the trees "to give us more time tomorrow." (He has decided to let his helpers be on their own on another job tomorrow, so the saved time will be valuable.)

He always begins by sharpening the chain saw. He seems painfully slow and methodical, filing alternate points in one direction, making the angles of the cutting edges of the teeth exactly parallel. Then the saw is turned and the process repeated for the alternating set of saw teeth facing the other direction. It only appears tedious and slow; actually Leroy is precise and sure of his movements; others take longer, are less careful and effective. His Swedish-made chain saw, used heavily day after day, invariably is in good working order when those of his helpers break down or balk.

We walk through brush and slash of earlier cuts to the first felling place. A few Norway tower over us, deepening the forest shadows in late day; young spruce and pine — released, sunlighted, nourished by the earlier harvest — are already asserting dominance over wild raspberry and hazel brush.

Leroy yanks the roaring chain-saw motor to life,

steps up to the first spruce, and with quick slashes cuts the lower limbs from the trunk. He glances up, once again taking measure of the crowns and branches of adjacent trees, then cuts the *kerf* — the wedge on the side toward which the tree would fall — so that the kerf angle and slant will control the direction of the fall. Height, depth, and angle of kerf are chosen by taking into account wind direction, natural lean of the tree, and its center of gravity.

He circles the tree, sets the saw a couple of inches above the kerf and on the opposite side. The motor roars, saw chips fly in competition with deerflies and mosquitoes. The smell of gas and oil fumes obliterates other odors. A few more seconds and the old spruce leans, topples, crashes to the ground, its clusters of top-branch cones kissing the earth; the butt recoils once from the contact, then comes to rest. The cutting had taken a minute at most; the open skies now mark space formerly taken by the spruce.

Leroy limbs it while I examine the butt. This tree had been struck by lightning years before — scoring half the trunk to a depth of an inch; the tree had filled the scar with pitch and new growth that closed over most of it. But near the butt insects had found ingress, and their workings had admitted rot. The tree was sound from waist height up; its base had been mortally wounded.

I lay the 100-inch measuring stick, cut from an aspen sapling, against the now-cleared trunk, and Leroy marks the cuts. A few minutes more and the spruce is cut into lengths, the branches pulled into slash rows. We go on to the next.

We cut ten. The rest will come down tomorrow.

Cutting is done by midmorning. It doesn't take long to lay down a tree, even in heat, amid insects. The heavy work begins then: end-over-ending or tossing the cut lengths to be within reach of the Cat as it snakes and clanks between the pines.

Leroy pulls up to one of our hand-assembled piles, parks, swivels in his seat, and operates the multiple levels of the jammer. His calloused hands have a light touch, a harp player's finesse, as he manipulates the jaws, loosening their bite from the radiator cap (their regular anchoring place when the Cat is in motion). Like huge hydraulic ice tongs, or a giant's fishing-pond toy, the jammer jaws open, close and clamp on the logs, and stack them according to Leroy's commands. Then the arm swings out. The jaws open, drop on the pile, pick up two or three sticks, hoist them, stack them neatly on the skid hitched behind the Cat. Leroy loads neatly; he adroitly uses the jammer jaws to move one stick forward, another back, until they end exactly aligned, so the cut ends make a perfect plane. It's the same with picking them up: he rolls sticks aside to get one he wants to fill a hole, or to arrange pulp on the bottom and bolts on top in order to make off-loading more efficient.

As soon as the skid is loaded we head for the yard, where the three piles are growing: sawlogs, bolts, and pulpwood. I accompany the Cat and skid on foot, and Leroy calls out to me, "There's a stick over there we'll pick up with the next load of bolts!" He points and I nod, although I don't see the stick he is talking about. He seems to have a photographic memory of each tree and the several sticks cut from it, and which of the several sticks is ordained for a sawlog, a bolt, or pulpwood.

It is tiring work aggravated by the biting insects and by the heat, but like all such work it is pointless to take too many rest breaks. That only prolongs the job. We keep at it, finally dragnetting the last stick, and by early afternoon there is the relative luxury and ease of loading the truck from the three piles in the yard, and then hauling to town to the buyers. We are done by five.

Leroy took the first load into town at lunch; he needed to pick up some tractor parts at the same time. The next load, at two, was sawlogs to a local mill that paid top prices (as had the pulpwood commission agent for the papermill). Leroy knows all the buyers, and who is paying how much each day, and what they need. The last load of bolts goes to the big buyer who had run the newspaper ad. Checks are made out to each of us, the price divided evenly. It comes to about $200 apiece, for all the sales combined — not much, considering the work, the equipment, the know-how furnished by Leroy; the work and the trees by me.

It's better this way than to let the trees die a lingering death, ultimately useless except as organic matter.

And the $200 will pay for ten thousand seedlings next spring.

Paul's been here two days, camping at his favorite spot, on the hill between the two lakes. He claims he does this because his two dogs are a nuisance around the house, and one of them tends to be sharp with the younger children. Part of it is his love of the hill; even as a boy he would go there for his private times.

Paul looks sober, preoccupied, as we hike along together. I ask, "What's bothering you?"

He doesn't want to say, finally blurts, "It looks so awful with the spruce gone."

"I know it."

"And it's the same with where you cut the jack pine and aspen last year," he goes on. "Smith and Derek don't even want to come here, it looks so bad."

"But they did come and helped replant it."

"Well yes, we all did. But it was a shock seeing how it looked. All the big trees gone and the slash on the ground turning brown."

"The slash is already becoming invisible, overgrown and decomposing. And the new trees we planted are coming up."

"I know. We all know it had to be done. We know that the jack pine and aspen were scrub stuff and needed to come out to make room for better trees. It's just that it looks so different, awful."

It's hard to accept that the sacred places of childhood undergo change. The old schoolroom revisited seems small, no longer overwhelming; the old teacher, once so imposing and powerful, seems diminutive and seems to have problems and cares of his own. You may look backward, but you cannot go home again.

"It takes some getting used to," I say. "Let's take a walk."

The dogs bound and race around us, a pair of German shepherds Paul has had since they were puppies. They are over two years old and complicate his living arrangements by making it difficult to find a tolerant landlord. We watch the dogs enjoy the running room, the space, but we are alert to possible encounters with skunks, which are plentiful. The female shepherd has a propensity for getting too close and was thoroughly sprayed last spring. Exiled, she howled, circled the house, and shared the odor through the open window. Then the male, inspecting the cause of her unhappiness, rubbed against her and came back into the house to tell us about it.

"I can tell from her bark when she scents one," Paul declares hopefully.

"It's one of the ways," I say, dubiously.

We reach the top of the hill, where Paul's mountain tent is pitched. Once again I am surprised by the absence of the big spruce, by the difference in silhouette and in spacial relationships.

"It's hard for me to get used to," I tell Paul. "Every time I come here I'm surprised and I want to call out 'Hey, who cut these trees?' "

We walk beyond his neat campground, making our way through the woods. The old paths are impassable

because of the slash, and we find different routes. At
the end of the hillcrest, where it slopes to the marsh
leading to the river, we sit on a spruce stump. This had
been one of the sentinel trees, marking the farthest
advance of the woods toward the river. It had been a
landmark during hunting, for rendezvous for lunch
when working among the trees, a place to put clues
during treasure hunts. The stump provides ample
space for both of us to sit; there is even room for one
or two more people.

We sit in silence. This is comfortable for us and
conversation is by fits and starts when Paul and I are
together. Talk interpersed by pauses and quiet times
because the tempo of our minds is much alike and we
are often attuned. On the other hand, we can talk by

long distance phone and find it hard to terminate a conversation.

Downhill are the rotting remnants of another large spruce, a twin to the sentinel, blown over during a storm a few years before. It too had blocked then-familiar paths and necessitated new ones for animals and for ourselves. It was this casualty that had caused me to consider, reject, reconsider the need to cull the trees.

"This stump is pretty rotten at the center," Paul says.

I nod, then ask, "Remember when we tried to plant the sidehill with the planting machine?"

"I sure do." Paul laughs. "Second or third year. I was on the planter with you and Smith was driving the tractor. The planter tipped over a couple of times. Guess we should have planted by hand."

"The trees took pretty well. Shall we walk that way?"

"Okay."

8

Ricing

THE WILD-RICE HARVEST will open August 23, a week from now. It's a tentative date, of course, because weather conditions can delay the final ripening, and the Wild Rice Committee of the Minnesota Chippewa tribe, which has jurisdiction over all waters within the boundaries of the reservations, makes the final decision. The state conservation department follows suit for the public waters outside the reservations.

I'm fond of the rice, as is Peggy. But I like the harvesting and she does not. As a child growing up on Leech Lake Reservation she had to participate in the harvest. It was a matter of survival, of enough food for the family, of enough cash income for school clothes and family needs in the fall. For many families it was the major or only source of cash income during the year. Later, when she had completed high school and gone on to nurse's training, she had gone ricing to earn tuition, money for clothing and for books.

When she was twelve she had been caught in a wild storm crossing Lake Winnibigoshish with a day's harvest in a skimpy, tippy skiff. Water washed over the six-inch-high sides of the flat-bottomed boat, the paddle broke, the long ricing pole was less than worthless — a hindrance really. Her partner was a young girl also, and the two children struggled against waves and wind, separated from the family and the accompanying boats by the storm. They made shore after hours of struggle, found shelter with an old recluse who fed them hot homemade vegetable soup.

Ricing has its grim side apart from economic necessity. There are drownings, mishaps, accidents; and in some small towns and villages there is police harassment of Indian ricers: speed traps are set up just then to cash in on the earnings, because it is one of the few times of the year when many people have ready money to pay fines; it is also as a consequence a time of year when there is talk in the Indian communities of police brutality — prisoners beaten in jail and women abused by the predominantly white police. The sharp upsurge in contact between white police and Indian ricers aggravates the unresolved conflicts and otherwise sublimated or sidestepped passions. Above all, for those to whom ricing means income and food, it represents physical exertion beyond belief — fighting wind; getting through boggy, low water; and just plain getting to and from the fields.

It isn't even rice, if you want to be technical about it, but a form of wild oat — rich in protein, indestructible if properly stored. Wild rice is said to be the only

undomesticated grain in the world; no scientist has yet
been able to breed a strain that is nonshattering — the
prime requirement of domestication. *Shattering* refers
to the hundred or so seed grains at the head of the stalk
ripening at different times and then falling off, instead
of all ripening at once as they do in domesticated
grains. A poetic justice — symbolic, I think — that the
staple food of woodland Indians has resisted domestication. In parts of the world, other "wild" grains are still
harvested: emmer, a variety of wheat; rye; sorghum, in
various forms; teosinte, an early form of corn. But they
actually have been tamed, domesticated — the original
shattering characteristic bred out of them even though
the source forms of the grains are still used. Wild rice
has not been so altered. Yet.

There are places not far from our farm where the
ancient rice caches of the Indians can still be seen —
the vestiges of the camping, hunting, trapping life of
centuries until the last. They appear as pits in the
ground, usually near hillsides and old camping sites.
They used to be several feet deep, stone-lined, carefully constructed to stay dry. Rice stored there would
keep for years. Now the pits are merely circular inden-
tations, but our children have seen them and know
what they are and what they represent.

By law and by preference we harvest in the traditional Indian way — by canoe. One person stands in
the stern using a sixteen-foot spruce pole to push
through the waters of the lakes and rivers where the
rice grows wild. The other harvester sits or kneels at
the poler's feet and "knocks" the rice.

There's an art to poling, to keeping the canoe moving steadily and not jerkily, to keeping it in the rice
fields among the reedy-looking stalks rising five or six
feet above the water that varies from a few inches to
several feet deep. There's skill also in traversing the
rice fields so as to do minimum damage to the plants,
saving them for a second round at a later time.

But there's an art to knocking, too. With a stick in
each hand (the sticks are up to thirty inches long and
an inch thick at the handle, and taper to a point) you
reach out with one as the canoe glides through the
rice, bend the gathered stalks over the canoe, and
stroke the heads with the end of the other stick. The
ripe kernels fall into the bow of the canoe. If you do it
right, the milky, unripe grains remain behind on the
stalk to be knocked, or rapped, another day. Then you
reach out on the other side, bend stalks and heads over
the canoe, knock the stalk heads with the free stick.
When you start in the morning you can hear the ripe
grains rattle into the bottom of the canoe. As the day
goes on the sound becomes softer and softer as grain
falls on grain, and finally there are only the swish-
swish sound of the knocker's stick against sheaves, the
drip-drip from the pole, and a splash as the pole is
reset. The canoe fills with rice — with the long,
barbed beards at the tip of the grains up, the heavier
grain ends down — until there is a fuzzy green-brown
blanket of hair stretching out before the knocker in the
canoe.

The beards shatter and break; pieces get into clothes
and all over the body, crawling there propelled by tiny

barbs. A piece of broken rice beard in the eye can mean serious problems, and many knockers wear sunglasses as protection. In addition to broken rice beards, small light beige worms about an inch long drop off the plants, into the canoe, and get into clothing, adding to the discomfort.

Preparing for a harvest, I check the canoe and the sixteen-foot-long pole. Sometimes the end of the pole, shaved thin and slipped into a metal duckbill, has become weakened and cracks. It's wise to check beforehand and not get out in the rice fields, miles from the landing, to then discover a broken pole. The first year Peggy and I riced together, the end of the pole broke off in the middle of a field, leaving the duckbill caught behind in the muck.

"Oh, let's quit, we've got enough," Peggy said.

"We don't either." (I've never got enough rice.) "I'm going after that duckbill."

"In this muck? How deep is it?"

I stripped to my shorts and lowered myself into the water. Toes touched silt three feet down and kept sinking, another foot and a half, two feet.

"Going swimming?" one of Peggy's cousins called over from a nearby canoe. "I thought you were going ricing."

"Did you lose a grain?" the other cousin called over solicitously.

A duckbill costs several dollars, but even more important is the time it saves, because without the device the pole is useless. One either has a pole with a forked stick fastened at the end to set against the submerged tufts of stalks and roots at the bottom, or a metal duckbill which spreads against the roots and springs together when the pole is pulled back out. Without either a fork or a duckbill, the sixteen-foot pole would sink into the silty lake bottom.

I groped in the mud with my feet, finally felt the duckbill and dove to retrieve it. Back in the canoe, I was covered with black ooze and silt.

I wanted no repeat performances this time. I checked the knocker sticks, the regular pair and the extras; they can break, too, after years of use. Car carriers and straps, equipment all ready — now we have to check the fields.

Checking is a special occasion. You drive backroads rarely taken otherwise; look for partridge and deer signs on the way, as well as for signs of next year's berry prospects; keep an eye out for wild grapes, for bittersweet for Christmas. It's a time when mosquitoes and deerflies are gone and wood ticks all but forgotten — a sweet time made richer by the prospect of harvest. Harvesters all have their own places to check, their own bellwethers, like old-timers forecasting weather. It's probably unnecessary to go out and do this checking, but it's so much fun.

"Mom says she heard it looks pretty good in Sucker Bay, but it's not ripe yet," Peg says.

"That one's usually a week late."

"The committee will have a special opening date there. Let's look at Ravens Lake."

For weeks we've been watching the rice: first, in early July, it looks like grass floating in the water, and later, like spears standing up; it grows to full height in August, heading out in mid-August; and then the grains fill out. We have our favorite ricing places along the river, or Steamboat Creek. Progress there is a fairly reliable index to conditions elsewhere. We've never riced Ravens Lake together (Peg had been there as a child); and we'd never been out on Sucker Bay together either (which is where I had riced occasionally in years before our marriage). But then, ricing is one thing, checking another.

"You don't have the knockers and the pole along?" Peggy asks. Game wardens check closely for preseason harvesting and there is a fine and possible confiscation of equipment, canoe, or even car, for violators.

"Just the paddles." The lightweight sixteen-foot canoe, which replaces a much heavier and clumsier eighteen-foot freighter type I used to own, rides easily atop the car.

"Too bad we won't have any company this year." A family joke; both of us smile. Some years before, city friends vacationed with us during ricing preparations. Deciding that it couldn't be so difficult, my friend fixed a pole and knockers for himself and his wife and said they also would harvest rice on opening day. That season opened amid cold, chilly overcast as we put our canoes in at a lake a few miles from the farm. Our two canoes set off amid a small flotilla heading for the field a mile upshore. My friend set his pole and pushed off with the rest, but a quarter mile out he "caught a crab" — his pole became stuck in the weeds. We watched in disbelief as he stood in the stern of his canoe, his hands at the very end of the sixteen-foot pole, tugging to free the other end from its entanglement. The canoe slid forward; for an instant he was left clutching the pole, his knees pulled up under him as the canoe slipped out and away, carrying his wife. He hung suspended over the water, then sank majestically, in slow motion, and disappeared under the surface. He came up spluttering and they returned to shore. They drove back for a change of clothes and rejoined us later, but somehow the steam had gone out of their ricing.

Those for whom ricing is vital would never have lost the precious hours to get a change of clothing. Wet, cold, whatever: the hours of harvest are limited, curtailed by necessary regulation. If you want it, you have to get out there and knock it. Peg knew that well; so in my own way did I, because there were years for me, too, when I had to knock rice and sell it to live.

Today's scouting was inconclusive. The fields looked good, thick in spots, but as usual, many grain husks were still empty this early, and the full ones yielded test grains still milky and white inside.

We munched a few grains on the way home — a mealy taste, only faintly reminiscent of the nutty flavor of finished wild rice.

"Tastes good," we agree. By-products of the day: a basketful of wild grapes, a harmless encounter with a mother skunk and five playful little ones, and a notation on the location of bittersweet for harvest closer to Christmas time.

The big rice fields are still closed, not quite ripe. Allowing canoes into such fields now would result in broken, kinked, mashed-down stalks that could never rise erect again. After one pass by scores of canoes the field would be ruined. The committee has closed the fields, posted notices, and stationed tribe members at the accesses. It'll be day to day until a decision is made to open one, then another. Many people are disappointed, particularly those who have come home from city jobs for a few days of ricing and have to be back before the big fields open. However, the smaller lakes and rivers are ready, and everybody converges on them. It's where we usually go for reasons of proximity, familiarity, and a tradition of sorts. The rice tends to be small-grained in rivers and small lakes, but it's as tasty as the large-grained — in my opinion at least. Today it was crowded, one canoe next to another, and I doubt that the field will recover for a second, much less a third round.

Peg's folks didn't come. They're wise and experienced enough to anticipate the crowding and the mayhem. Peg says they are perfectionists. When they rice there is never a whole head knocked into the canoe, never a stalk. It is perfect rice — clean, only ripe grains — and harvested with a minimum of damage to the stalks. Whenever a canoe or skiff passes through a rice field, the resulting scene always looks as though a dinosaur had wallowed there, sliding through and breaking plants in both directions. But a good poler can keep the damage to a minimum and a good knocker can feel the right degree of bending and knocking that will garner only ripe grains and not damage the remainder of the stalks. Peg's folks are good. We are middling good. A lot of people out today showed no respect for the rice, smashing their way through regardless of damage, harming the rice bed to the point where ungarnered rice and stalks were pounded into the water never to rise again. We saw people knocking heads and stalks into their canoes, to be pushed and crammed into sacks at the end of the day and sold to the buyers who wait at the landings, with scales on their trucks.

There are many stories about how buyers are swindled by harvesters. It's a game more widely joked about than actually practiced. But buyers are thought of as moneyed people, though most of them buy with money furnished by the processors or distributors. Buyers keep the price down, sometimes pocketing the few-cents-a-pound difference between what they pay harvesters and what they collect from their employers. Buyers are the enemy. So rice sacks are soaked in water prior to weighing to add a pound or two, or sometimes have a turtle in them, or rocks.

Once I heard a buyer complain about it: "I don't mind so much getting cheated; it happens once in a while. But the other night I was dumping out sacks I'd bought in the afternoon and inside one sack was a folded-up winter overcoat with just a little bit of rice on top of it. You know, that coat looked damned familiar. I looked at it and looked at it, and finally I took it in the house and asked Mary to look at it, and she says, 'that looks like your coat that I hung out on the line to air.' So she looks in the backyard and the coat is gone. They sold my own coat back to me, that's what hurts."

Cheating the buyers is not only a class war of poor against rich, of exploited against exploiters; it's also for some people a rebellion against having to sell the rice at all rather than keep and use it themselves. Poverty and commercialization combine into an economic necessity. It is a categorical imperative that breeds loathing. It's sad. Understanding what's happening doesn't make it less sad. I think back on my own feelings and attitudes the first two years, when I had to sell my rice and could afford to keep only a little of it. My whole approach and actions then had been different than they are now, when I can rice for myself.

I still feel embarrassment and a tinge of shame when I think of the time I put my foot on the scale while one of my rice bags was being weighed by the buyer and hiked the weight by sixteen pounds. In those days the buyers paid twenty-five to thirty-five cents per pound of green rice, and the finished rice sold in big-city stores for three and four dollars a pound. My partner that year thought this was great and kidded me about my "golden foot." It bothered me and I took another sixteen pounds of green rice to the buyer sometime later. He was surprised and said he hadn't even noticed and would never have missed it — he bought mar⌐ thousands of pounds each year. My partner thought I was crazy. But I had a low opinion of this particular buyer-distributor because of his shabby business practices — his profiteering, his extension of credit during the year and loan of ricing boats to the poor in return for agreement on their part to sell exclusively to him, sometimes at lower prices than others were paying. I didn't want to be like him.

We've skipped ricing the last few days. It's been permitted for half-days only, on alternating days. Yesterday was an off day, and I checked around and found a good patch. Nobody's been in it. Hard to get to but worth the effort.

We're off early this morning, carrying lunch, coffee thermos, and a jug of juice. It's cold out, close to frost. Overhanging aspen shading the old logging road are turning color. Here and there a splash of red as maple turn, offset by pine green, aspen yellow. It smells like fall, wisps of pungent, wet acid odors are in the moist air.

"Some year we should live out at a sugar camp in spring," Peg says. "The boys ought to experience an old-time maple-sugar harvest." Few old-timers still camp out in the woods at sugar time, just as very few finish their rice the old way.

We bump along the road, wondering whether anyone else will be in this remote place. At the end of the road there is another car; its occupants are ahead of us and out of sight. We unload, portage canoe and gear through wet and marshy trail half a mile. Finally it gets too wet, becomes marsh but is not deep enough to pole. I swing the canoe off my back, Peg stows gear, and I pull while Peg pushes. We're wet above our knees, partway to our thighs, and it's cold. Then there is enough water and we get in the canoe and begin to pole. It's very hard poling; we go aground on humps of bog, are back in deeper water, go aground again. Finally, deeper water. It's a mile to the rice.

Coots fly up, settle a few feet ahead, fly up again. So do sora rails, shy sandpiper-like birds that feast in the fields. A pair of blue-winged teal. An American bittern flies up, startles us; we had been within ten feet and had not seen it. Then we approach the field. The other canoe is already there; I can see shoulders and head of the poler, flashes of the movement of his arms — about half of the pole sticking up above the rice as he sets it, then its slant, its gradual disappearance as he pushes it hand over hand. In a big rice field like Sucker Bay, that's all you see of the other ricers — just the poles sticking up and slanting down, like distant matchsticks. Today there are only two of us here in this small spot. Good.

The other poler is a cousin of Peg's and we recognize each other, wave with a free hand as we hand-over-hand on our poles. There's no shouted greeting today, although we get raucous at times; somehow the silence and the perfection of the day disinvite immediate hellos, and we will meet sooner or later anyway, when we make our turns at the end of the field to reenter it on a parallel course. We do this and avoid crisscrossing because it makes for easier ricing and saves more of the plants. We'll pull alongside each

other during lunch break — that's taken for granted, and needs not be said.

Stalks and rice heads are dew-soaked. The rice doesn't fall as well when it is wet — the stems and heads tend to break off more easily. But the first few strokes bring a rattle of ripe grains into the canoe. What a lovely sound! Visions of wild-rice hot dish, of rice and venison. And just the sound, the ethos, satisfy. I no longer think about how much we will harvest today. The *doing* is all I want at this moment.

My vista is of green-beige rice for over half a mile ahead. On my left the uneven contour of higher land — brush- and tree-covered, fading into marsh and then water. There are cattails over there, and I peer around for signs of cranberries but see none. On my right is the little river, which has widened out to become half river, half lake at this place. The field is narrow — perhaps three hundred feet wide — and long. This allows long swaths, then turnaround at the end, reentry, and another long swath. The other canoeist and I silently divide the turf — he taking the outside, nearest the river; I taking the inside, nearest the shore. There's enough for both of us. There's an occasional bump and splash as his pole or mine scrapes the canoe. When we pass close to each other I hear the swish-swish of the knocker in the other canoe. Peg's cousin Dickie and I smile at each other as we pass.

Before me Peg's thin, long arms flash out in steady rhythm. She looks and moves much as her mother does at times like this. The rice is covering the canoe bottom, beards sticking up like a miniature forest, and there is only an occasional rattle as grains fall against the canoe sides. Some grains fall into the water, a lot of them really, as the canoe nudges stalks and as the knockers reach out. Food for ducks, for other wildlife; seeds for future plants. Such seeds float toward the bottom, bury themselves in the silt helped by the barbed beards. They may rest there for many years before germinating, for the outer husk is remarkably tough; the silicate compound goes through repeated freezing and thawing before it cracks, admits water to the inner core, and thereby permits the seed to become viable.

The long pole gets wet, drips. I invariably get wet and sometimes water drips on Peg. This is annoying and I resolve to try harder. Peg's father, lean and long-armed, is a fastidious poler who never gets wet, never drips on the knocker. It's a hard skill to match, as hard as her mother's flawless knocking.

We take a midmorning break in the pleasant sunshine, the two canoes side by side. Dickie's partner, not visible until now, turns out to be another cousin, Beryl. The two knockers stand up, brush off rice grains and beards, stretch.

"Careful, Peggy," Dickie warns. "I still remember the time you tipped all the canoes! Remember?"

We laugh at the familiar story, although it was a friend of Peg's who did the actual tipping during a midmorning break much like this one. There had been several canoes side by side, and Peg's partner — another nursing student — made an awkward move, tipped over the canoe; then one after the other they all tipped in a chain reaction. Some rice was lost, all lunches got wet, and for the rest of the day a careful eye was kept to find out who had dry cigarettes.

"I'm watching, Dickie. How're you and the game warden getting along these days?" Dickie has been known to jump the season by a few days now and then, and there are tales of his being chased by the wardens, of hairbreadth escapes, and of getting caught a few times.

We resume ricing. It is hot now, the skies are clear, and before we know it, it is noon and the deadline has come. We head back to the landing reluctantly, knocking rice as we go. Then comes the poling through the bog — harder now that the canoe is weighted by

the rice. We drag and push; get to the landing wet,
panting, exhausted; and sack the rice.

Sitting on the ground before driving home, Dickie
says, "This ought to be good for another round in a
few days."

"About a week?"

"About."

He shot a deer a few days before. As a tribe member
he is eligible to hunt on the reservation during the
tribally set season, which is longer than that controlled
by the state, off the reservation. "We'll stop over with a
roast," he promises. When we've got, we share. It's
comfortable.

"Who's finishing your rice?" Dickie knows we don't
sell.

"I do it myself at Gafe's mill."

We help each other load the canoes atop the cars
and part.

Gafe runs one of several small processing mills in
the area. It's in a large, garagelike shed, well·venti-
lated. The rice is roasted in large rotating drums; a
wood fire underneath is kept at a steady burn. Once
roasted golden brown, and cooled, the rice is threshed
in a different drum, this one anchored but with rotating flails inside. The threshing removes the now-
golden husks, and after being winnowed and having
the chaff removed, the brown-black kernels are ready
to package, store, cook, eat. Roasting and threshing are
tricky, persnickety. The rice must not be roasted too

much or it will burn and not taste good, but if not roasted enough the hulls don't come off. It must not be threshed too much or the protein-rich outside layer is polished off. Gafe is a master at it. He's gangly, stubble-faced, in his sixties (he claims, though it could be his seventies); and he lost one arm many years ago. Yet he runs the plant, stokes the fires, tends the machines, tests roasters and threshers like a French pastry chef. I've seen him load roasters with a scoop shovel, but I still can't explain just how he does it.

I've been taking my rice to Gafe's since my third year of ricing, not only because the rice is finished well under Gafe's supervision, but because he humors me and lets me finish my own rice. He keeps a close eye on what I do and makes the decisions on when the roasting is done ("Well, it tastes all right, you can dump it now," he says, cracking a test kernel between sparse yellowed teeth). Threshing requires an even greater watchfulness. The boundary between enough threshing and polishing-off nutrients is a narrow one.

There is a mix of several very distinct smells. The predominant smell of roasting is not so much the smoke odor from the wood fire (which pervades everything and is shoved subliminally into the background) as it is the increasing pungency of the moisture evaporating from the nutmeglike wild rice. The threshing produces a dry, sandlike chaff — almost a dust — high in silica content, that smells like ground straw. Some people wear face masks covering nose and mouth; others chew tobacco. (Once I saw Gafe wearing a face mask. When he saw me looking he pulled it aside and said, "My wife makes me wear it to keep from talking," and put it back on.)

At the end of the process a fanning mill separates chaff from grain and the precious rice is funneled into containers. Some people prefer heavy-gauge plastic sacks placed inside white cloth sacks to make fifty- and hundred-pound lots. I myself like the cylindrical cartons — heavy cardboard with metal tops and bottoms — holding forty or fifty pounds each, depending on carton size. To each his own.

"I see you got some more of that puny river rice," Gafe greets me. "Whyn't you get some of that good rice up to Inger and Squaw Lake?"

He likes the larger-kernel rice; it's easier to roast and thresh.

"This is tastier," I reply. We have the same conversation at least once each season.

"That's what they all say," he shrugs his resignation. "Over there." His armless sleeve indicates a roaster and I set to work dumping my sacks, shoveling the green rice into the roaster.

"That's wet. Couldn't you cure it a little more?"

"And let it mildew?" We set to work. It takes all morning and I listen to Gafe as he taunts and jibes others who come for custom-processing. A lot of people finish their own rice, keep some of it, sell the rest to tourists. But most harvested rice goes to large processors, whose agents and buyers are found at every canoe landing.

The tribe has gone into the rice business in recent years, including the establishment of large artificial paddies on Leech Lake Reservation. The paddies are seeded in spring, flooded, and the water level controlled. Before harvest they are drained, dried; then combines harvest the rice. But this is in the paddies only — the wild stands are harvested by canoe. The experiment seems to be working out after several years of operation, and there is consideration of expansion and possibly building a tribal processing plant.

It is possible to increase the percentage of seed viability considerably by freezing the seed to minus-fifteen degrees Fahrenheit, and then thawing and refreezing it several times before planting, thus weakening the outer hull so that it will crack and admit water when sown, and germinate. In natural stands seeds may rest on lake bottoms several years and go through several winters before this happens. Also, University of Minnesota scientists and others are developing new seed strains to reduce shattering. Some day even this last undomesticated grain will bow to man's penchant for domination. Then, I suppose, it will be planted by the Minnesota Chippewa tribe in its paddies.

My rice is finished. It's a piddling amount by Gafe's standards, but he knows what it means to me. Two hundred twenty-five pounds of green rice produced a hundred pounds of finished rice — a very high yield ratio, because usually it runs one pound finished from three pounds green. The rice must have been ripe, with a minimum of milky grain, broken stalks, and heads.

"Some year you'll learn how to knock rice," Gafe says sadly. "And get some larger stuff next time." Then he grins, I pay, and take my leave. It costs fifteen cents to twenty cents a pound to process rice.

The big processors usually calculate the costs per pound of finished wild rice as follows:

3 lbs. green at 50¢ per lb. to the harvester	$ 1.50	
Transportation	.15	
Commissions	.15	
Processing and packaging	.20	
	$ 2.00	total, per lb.

In years when the harvest is poor the price of a pound of green rice will fluctuate to over one dollar a pound; it doesn't happen very often. When it does, there usually isn't enough rice in the fields to make the harvesting worthwhile. The harvesters pay their own gas and oil, invest their own time, and hope for the best. Good harvesters can make money during the season, especially if the whole family participates. Young children stay home to babysit even younger ones; older children harvest. The schools are furious, and sometimes penalize absentees for reporting a week or two late in September — and that's a source of community friction. The schools accommodate the farm and resort ethos by letting out early in May so students can help out at home; the same consideration is not always given to those who have to help rice. Our community doesn't always acknowledge the economics of Indian life and culture; it seeks to impose its own values — in the land taken from the Indians.

On the way home from Gafe's I stop at Buck Lake to visit Charles Nordhall, whom I want to enlist to help me with some carpentry work. There is a fire going in the yard overlooking the lake. A huge iron kettle is over the fire and rice is roasting, being stirred with a canoe paddle. It's being finished the old way — and I wish Tony and David were with me.

A pit dug in the ground is lined with rawhide. A diagonal pole is extended across the pit — one end fastened to the ground, the other end resting on a forked stick about three feet high. Traditionally rice is threshed by one person jigging on the roasted rice in the pit. Moccasin leather against roasted rice — it is a gentler, more finely tuned threshing than that done by today's machinery, and there are songs and dance steps about it.

Someone is winnowing the rice in a flat woven basket, flipping a small amount of threshed rice and chaff in the air, catching the grains in the basket while the breeze blows the chaff away.

I sit on the ground with Charles, watching the roasting, jigging, and winnowing, drinking in the smells of wood fire and roasting rice in the clear, cool air. No machinery noise, no exhaust fumes. Just good earthy smell, comfortable companionship. I forget about my errand and Charles doesn't ask; he's probably guessed, and we both know it has to wait until after ricing.

At home I unload the rice and Peg runs her hands through it, smells it, chews a few grains.

"Good rice," we agree.

I fetch a small sack of green rice I've held back, a

few handfuls, and get a bucket of clay from the trunk of the car.

"When did you get that?" my wife asks.

"The other day when I went out to check the river," I say.

We make clay balls, about two inches in diameter, imbedding a few grains of ripe green rice in each. When we are done there is a pail full of clay balls. I take the canoe down to the little lake, and set about the seeding. The clay will drop to the bottom, dissolve slowly and release the seeds, tending to protect the grains from ducks and other wildlife.

We've been doing this almost every year, and there is a green and beige fringe of rice growing around the little lake in the midst of the tree plantation. We keep seeding it, letting it take hold, and somehow never think of harvesting it: it's too sparse, too fragile yet. That's what we say. What we feel is that harvesting the little lake would denigrate the act of offering.

9

Work Bee

IT'S UNUSUALLY COLD, clammy September weather. Foggy and hazy outside, the wood stove going inside, condensation gathering on the window panes. I spent most of the day into the evening at the Jamison place, but there was little for me to do.

Curtis Jamison arrived here with wife and his family last fall, only a year and a half after we moved here. He is not the first successful midwest farmer to sell out and give in to the magic of the north country. We had little in common save the mystique of the north. He was a hunting and fishing enthusiast who considered traditional farming a means to that end, and we had followed our disparate visions to the same township.

His wife Mabel is full-bodied and getting heavy — an attractive kewpie face, vivacious. She covets life in town and wants to run a seamstress shop as she had done before they married. The three daughters are between thirteen and sixteen — at the squirreliest age, of boys and boyfriends, of loathing the chores. The two sons are too young to help with the chores. Curtis is short — shorter than his wife — but wiry, bald, and helpless without glasses. A hardworking farmer, of the kind who succeed farther south and survive marginally in our harsh climate and thin soil.

At the last township meeting somebody said Curtis had paid Kansas prices for northern-Minnesota land, but that was before the Jamisons came in: loud, gregarious — the girls flocking to the other teenagers like starlings; the wife heading to the trestle table with their food share for the social hour, the little boys clutching her skirt; he to exchange tales with the other men about where the deer were running and what the fish were biting on, and to ask did I plan to go duck hunting and where. It hadn't taken long for them to become part of the life.

This forenoon his good friend and neighbor Max Fawcett had called, asking me over to Curtis's "right away, please." Such summons are rare and I said I'd come, no questions asked. Max had hosted Curtis and his family each summer for more than ten years; they came from the same county and had been boyhood friends. Then Curtis would also come and stay with Max during partridge season, again for deer season, and sometimes for the ducks. The chance of becoming neighbors again had much to do with Curtis's transplanting his family, apparently reaching the decision to sell out abruptly and without much thought and consideration for the practicalities. I mulled over all that while driving over: the love bond of men who grow up together and share their lives; the deepening value of friendship over the years as contemporaries slip away; the precious interweaving of children and grandchildren and expanding families with cousins and nieces and nephews. I tried not to think of what troubles I would find.

I arrived simultaneously with the sheriff and we nodded to each other, walking into the frame farmhouse. Curtis was on his back, his face covered with a bloody towel. He was lying in the archway between the combined dining-living room and the half-step leading up to the kitchen. Curtis's glasses, one lens broken, lay on the floor next to him.

Sheriff Tom gently removed the towel and we stared at the pale face. Someone had closed the eyes. The bullet had entered under the chin, leaving a tiny purple hole, and had emerged at the top of the bald head making a larger hole, about the size of a half-dollar. I looked away from the wound and its coagulating blood, its fragments of tiny bones and globules of brain. He's done it to himself, I thought; he's taken his life, ended his dream. Why? Financial troubles making the farm pay? Overextended on mortgages for machinery and livestock? Pressure from Mabel and the kids to give it up and move back? There'd been talk of that. But it isn't that simple. . . .

Max stands there — huge, barrel-chested, curly brown hair — his face blanched by shock, barely restraining tears. Mabel is beside him, her face still frozen by the incomprehensibility and suddenness of

it; she hasn't cried yet, I think. On the other side of
Mabel is Max's wife, Beulah, who for once isn't smok-
ing a cigarette. There is a nervous twitch around Beulah's eyes and she keeps close to Mabel. For a moment
I am struck by the height differences: giant Max, a
step down to the stocky Mabel, another step down to
the diminutive Beulah's mouse-brown head. Then
Mabel says:

"That goddamned fox killed sixteen chickens day
before last!" Disasters were always befalling them, as
though a rain cloud had fastened above their heads
when they moved, never to leave. Their livestock sick-
ened when no one else's did; the brand-new machinery
broke down.

"We're outside this morning. It's cold and I'm helping him get the tractor backed up to the mower when
we hear the chickens. He run to the corner of the barn
and looks and says, 'It's the goddamn fox again.' So he
runs back t'the house for the twenty-two. His glasses
steamed up; it's hot in here and they was still steamed
up when I heard the shot and come in. He must've
tripped over the kitchen step. We didn't have no step
back home and he must've forgot. So he fell and it
went off." Then she yelled: "Goddamn stupid fox!"
And the tears came.

So he had died as impetuously as he had come to the
township.

I stay though there isn't much for me to do, because
they want me to. It's easier with several of us attend-
ing to what one person could really do because it
makes survival less lonely. But when I take my leave,

Max is on his hands and knees scrubbing the blood off the floor. He doesn't want any help with that chore and is sobbing, not wiping the tears. I see them fall on the floor and mix with the soapy water.

They're taking the body back south for burial, where they have a family plot. It's a big expense and they're already in debt, and it's unlikely that sale of the farm will cover the outstanding mortgage. But I don't know what I'm talking about; nobody's discussed the finances with me. I'm just feeling bad because it doesn't seem right that even in death he is denied his dream, his vision of his beloved north.

The Jamisons are back. They are trying to get the crops in. Last cutting of hay and the corn. It's not working out and Max is trying to help, but he's fighting this year's late season to get his own place in order. Last year when Fred, another neighbor, slipped a disk, his wife Susan climbed on the tractor and took over, and some of us came and helped as she directed. Mabel is different: social, cheerful, a great talker and an even greater cook, but not much good on a tractor or in the fields.

It's a bad time of the year for all of us. Farmers have to get crops in; everybody is busy. No one has much time to help the Jamisons. Yet they can't do it themselves; Mabel is trying, but that's the best that can be said. The girls help when they have to and try to enlist boyfriends, but there's no heart in it. Their crops *must* get in or they'll be losers for sure. Crops are needed for feed until the cattle and the pigs can be sold. None will be market-ready for another couple of months. I propose a work bee but Max is doubtful; the farmers are too broke to even scrape up the extra gasoline to keep machinery going. But there's no other solution. Max thinks the merchants won't help, and the farmers won't really turn out because Curtis was such a newcomer and few knew him — more a sports freak than a farmer. But we'll try.

I called at the radio station and the newspaper today. They'll help with publicity. Most merchants are noncommittal — sympathetic but not giving anything. Finally I score at the farm stores. One will donate a hundred gallons of gas, another some gas and oil; a cash donation at the third. In the afternoon some of the supermarkets come through with food donations — a case of bread at one, coffee and sugar at another. It all helps, but Max was partly right: few people know the family, and there is no real desire to help. Mainly they give to get rid of the solicitor.

"Who? Never heard of him. Oh, that one. Read about it. That sure was too bad. Well, if I start doing that, I'd have to do it for everybody. Oh, all right, all right, everybody doesn't have an accident and leave a young family and the crops standing in the field. All right, so the township is having a work bee. How about a bag of sugar and a quart of coffee cream? Don't mention it."

I must not be unreasonable just because I feel involved, feel touched. That doesn't mean everyone else has to. But I do wish for a greater feeling of community, of willingness to share grief and happiness and to become touched by the lives of others. We straight-arm others away too much — avoid them, don't let them come close, don't allow ourselves to be touched.

I hope for good weather Saturday. It's the best day, with youngsters out of school, and some of the high schoolers can help. Some adults with weekday town jobs might find it easier to come.

I stop to check with Max and Beulah. Max is out in his fields, working against time. He is behind in his work, having spent so much time at Curtis's. Beulah is on the phone, waving me in —

"Yeah, this Saturday." She lifts the ever-present cup of coffee toward her mouth — nodding at me to help myself to the coffeepot — and undangles the cigarette from her mouth at the instant the coffee cup arrives there. Through all this she doesn't stop talking. "Well, there's about seventy acres of hay to be gotten in and nearly a forty of corn. That's a lot, I know. Can you folks come and bring the tractor and the corn picker? Oh, lots of folks coming, but we really need you. Four-H is coming. Yeah, Farmers Union will help too."

I push a scribbled note under her nose and she nods, but keeps talking. "We'll have gas and oil there, so you don't need to bring. We'll have food too, but bring a hot dish. Okay, we'll count on you."

We talk for a while; she goes over her scorecard. A few "sure," most are "maybe," and only three definitely "no." The "no" replies are due to out-of-town engagements and heavy workloads. Beulah picks up the phone for the next call.

"Hi, Ellen, this is Beulah. D'you know the Jamisons? Well you heard what happened, yeah. Sure is too bad. Well listen, we're getting up a work bee Saturday, all day. Yeah, all their hay and corn needs to be brought in and Max thought if you all could come and bring your combine . . ." On the way out I hear her mention that we would have gas and oil; anything requiring a cash outlay is a problem for farmers.

Almost forgot. Since only a minority have telephones we'd discussed ways and means of reaching the ones without phones. I'd suggested that those with phones who agreed to come might go out to talk to their neighbors. But we finally decided that having a phone was unrelated to the degree of interest or commitment someone might have. A Farmers Union committee will go out and visit the families without phones. We won't know until Saturday what kind of turnout we will get.

I'm up at five, much too early; too nervous to sleep. It feels like it'll be a dreary, drizzly day. I go to town to pick up supermarket donations of bread, milk, coffee cream; and fresh breakfast rolls and donuts from the bakery — still oven-warm with pecan and cinnamon smells that tease my stomach. I stop at the radio station and they promise to broadcast reminders at intervals starting right now. They've been very good and helpful. I'm still worried about how many people will show. Mabel is up, cooking and baking with the oldest girl's help.

Out-of-town boyfriends are staying at the Jamisons and there's a heavy atmosphere. Somehow the girls' romances at this time seem cloying, disturbing under the circumstances. The constant hand-holding, petting, touching — unmindful of whoever is around — seems so incongruous. They're all ostentatious about it. I've seen this before and fail to understand it completely — this teenage reaction to the death or terminal illness of a parent. Reaction to the fear of death? To loss? It's like anger at being deserted. A plant or fruit picked before it is ripe will use its own inner resources and try to ripen prematurely, so that some of its seeds will be capable of germination. Humans, too?

A couple of tractors — one hauling combine and rake, the other a rake and a wagon — pull in shortly after eight. So does the one farm-store gas truck. We've arranged areas for equipment, fuel, repairs. Max is in charge of field work; myself logistics and organization. Beulah, Mabel, and my wife take charge of feeding. Coffee from a big urn and hot rolls are ready for all arrivals. There's to be plenty of food for midday and for a late-afternoon dinner; also midmorning and midafternoon snacks and juice.

It is cool, humid. There is a mist and it is overcast. Just such a morning as the one of Curtis's death. The yard explodes with clanking and noise as more tractors pull in. Cars are shunted to the field edge next to the barn. Within an hour the yard is almost empty: the tractors are in the field working almost side by side, one slightly behind the next, as they do in Montana

The noon meal is served in the front yard. Several large Norway pine tower over the white frame farmhouse, reminders of the forest that once was. On the front porch a serving table is improvised on trestles. Borrowed card tables and chairs dot the yard, but a lot of us sit or sprawl on the ground, eating with our backs propped against the trees. More chili, sandwiches, relishes, desserts than we can possibly eat, I think. But I've misjudged the appetites: the mountains of food disappear rapidly. There are nearly a hundred people now, from every nook and cranny of the township — most of them complete strangers to the Jamisons. We take heart from being together, doing a needed thing. Yet the adults are sober-faced — the older men in particular — everyone harboring their private thoughts about what had happened and why; and the men are preoccupied with the field work still to be done, with machinery breakdowns, broken sickle blades to be replaced on the mowers.

I'd been catching glimpses of my wife at the house; of Smith, Paul, and Derek working in the haymow, then once cleaning manure out of the barn. Now I see Smith being drafted to work in the hayfields along with some of the other older boys. Max is siphoning off the more experienced men to work the corn. It looks as if the clutch work will get done in good order: the hay in, the corn harvested and stored. But nobody is planning to leave; instead crews are organizing to do other necessary work. It's not life-and-death work, but necessary sooner or later on a farm, like cleaning manure out of the barn and spreading it on a newly tilled field.

A 4-H crew is getting ready to do just that, using tractor-pulled manure spreaders, but first the fields will have to be plowed and disked.

More people and machines are arriving now, and it's possible to bring machinery into the yard for repairs, substituting new arrivals. The haying is finished in midafternoon; some people prepare to leave.

"Stay for the dinner," Mabel pleads. "We got a real good dinner cooking."

"We'll go into town to shop and come back."

It has really dried off now, and dust rises from the fields as plows follow the harvesters. Behind the plows come the disks, then the harrows, then the manure spreaders. If Mabel keeps the farm, it will be ship-shape for spring planting. And if she decides to sell it, it will have the added value of being in good order for the next neighbors who join us.

I suddenly realize we have not kept a sign-in sheet; we have no way of knowing who is here or of sending thank-you letters. I also remember the camera and the promise to take pictures, and hasten out to the fields, noting that the light is getting poor for photography. When I get there the field work is done and I'm too late. But five tractors pulling flatbed wagons on creaky iron wheels are slowly rolling along. They are abreast, some distance apart. Behind the wagons is a long scraggly line of men, boys, girls. They are picking up fieldstones turned up by the plowing, piling them on the wagons. It's a chore Curtis Jamison had wanted to do and often talked about, but had not been able to get around to due to the pressure of more necessary

tasks — the survival needs of the farm. Now he is dead, and while no one has mentioned his name all day (as far as I could hear), the people of Frohn Township are honoring his desire. I put away the camera and join the line. Some stones are too big for one person to lift and we team up; a few boulders require three or four of us. I look up and find myself face to face with Paul — dusty and sweat-streaked — and we are both a little surprised and pleased. Grunt, heave, on to the next.

"Didn't think we'd get all that much done," Max says back at the yard. We are gathering for the dinner and some who'd gone shopping in town for their week's groceries are back, having brought ice cream for dessert.

"What happened out there?" I ask. "All we set out to do was bring in hay and corn and we thought we'd be lucky to get part of it done. We've gone way beyond."

Max says: "I don't know. It just kept going and

going. They're done plowing, disking, and harrowing. Spread what manure there was, enough for the small field."

Beulah — standing next to Max, taking a rest and puffing cigarette smoke — is puzzled too. (What a pair they are, standing there — nonsmoking Max, who is phlegmatic as a rule, and the intense bundle of nerves next to him.) She says: "Well I'm sure surprised so many turned out. Wanted to help the family, I suppose. It just kind of fell together."

The machines are all in; the gathering is a little easier. There's more talk, a little laughter here and there. We should be pleased, I think, but the mood is more one of fatigue and relaxation. Each of us would rather Curtis were here doing his own chores, no matter how satisfied we are that we could accomplish all this.

It's a great dinner. I have never seen the like except at the wakes for some of my Indian relatives, whose funeral feasts are an important tradition where hospitality is especially observed. At an Indian wake every relative, every friend brings a hot dish or other food: wild rice, venison, whatever food or gift that can be obtained. And so it is this late afternoon at the Jamison farm — except the people here are mostly Scandinavian, German, Irish, and English.

Evening slowly envelops us: an unspectacular, dreary twilight. The tractors and machinery are on the road in order to be home before nightfall; the yard empties. We stay to the end to help clean up, to take care of the last returns of borrowed card tables and chairs, coffee urns, some cooking utensils from nearby Township Hall. Then the kitchen is cleaned, the dishes washed, the leftover food distributed to departing families.

There is no way for Mabel to thank us, or for us to say we wish it hadn't had to be. So we say "we'll see you" and head home. The two younger girls and their beaus are in the house, but Mabel stands on the porch and waves, as does the oldest daughter, with her arm around her boyfriend.

"Mabel says she's definitely going to sell," my wife says. "Going back to Kansas and open a seamstress shop."

"I bet the girls are happy about that," Derek comments acidly. The boys tend to view the Jamisons' plans as disloyalty to the dead father. I don't. It's understandable — it was Curtis's dream, not theirs. Maybe with age the boys will think back on it more charitably, with more insight, and realize that dreams and desires are not always shared — that Mabel's

dreams of town life and her own business are as valid
to her as Curtis's dreams of living where he could hunt
and fish were to him.

The car smells of cow manure, grease, oil, dirt. We
pass the Jamison fence corner, a new cairn of freshly
picked fieldstones marking the boundary. I grieve that
a man who plunged his life savings to make a dream
come true couldn't savor it a little longer. And I'm
dismayed still that he plunged into his dying so reck-
lessly — an expert gun enthusiast tripping and falling
on his rifle! Was he subconsciously driven by his problems to court death? It's a nagging thought, pointless.

"A good crowd," I say. "Most of the township, and
some from outside."

In my mind's eye I see before me the long line of
volunteers stretched across the fields, reaffirming faith
in life and in each other by gleaning stones, and yes,
by marking respect to the man and his strivings in this
way. I think we all had come because we were needed
and because we need each other. It could have been
anyone in need, maybe ourselves. But mainly I think
we all came because we cared.

My mind's eye returns to the long line of gleaners. I
see ourselves in stop-action under the strobe light of
remembrance that illuminates our agonies; I see us
as caricatures, our jerky motions dancing out our
throes — for in a sense we are all victims of the plague
led by scythe-carrying death. Dance of death, dance of
life. It is an ancient conceit, for without life there cannot be death.

"Whose idea was it to pick the stones?" I ask. "Who started it?"

There is silence in the car, then Paul says: "Smith started it. So we did it. Nobody said anything; they just did it too."

10

A Matter of Respect

THE GROSS INCOME of the farm last year was $1,495 from sale of pulpwood, sawlogs, and bolts carefully selected and cut from the natural growth; none of it came from the newer plantations. The contract for sale of Christmas trees had been broken by the buyer, a wholesaler, at the last moment, and this was a double setback. It meant not only a financial disappointment, but it also delayed some necessary thinning of the plantation. To make matters worse, the sales agreement for live trees from the natural stand for landscaping was canceled by the golf club, which had to delay expansion plans indefinitely. The club wanted some fifteen- to twenty-foot-high birch and pine, which we have in abundance in some spots in the natural forest, and it wouldn't have hurt to thin those areas. We had worked out the technique of lifting those trees and moving them carefully — a particularly sensitive operation where birch are concerned. Now this agreement had fallen by the wayside as well.

We won't be heavily dependent on farm income until later in life when some of our earliest plantings are mature enough for selective cutting of posts and poles as part of an ongoing thinning operation. But the interim harvests (selling pulpwood, and replanting with better stock; thinning the plantation and selling by-products such as Christmas trees or posts and poles) improve the permanent stand, the density and quality of the remaining trees. So does the judicious culling and thinning of the natural stands. These are important for maintaining the growth and development of the farm and our ability to live there. We are in no position to heavily subsidize the ongoing planting and improvements, and we need the interim income to pay for seedlings and tree farm operations. Family living expenses are provided for by off-farm jobs that Peggy and I hold — which in my case have run the gamut from construction work, radio announcing, and school teaching, to training and executive management of Indian tribal enterprises, and ultimately senior federal government positions. Peggy's jobs have ranged from nursing, to health-program administration and direction, to her present law practice specializing in tribal law. Supporting ourselves is one thing; getting the tree farm to pay for itself, much less produce profit, is another. The economics of our way of life have proved an uneven course.

I've often asked myself whence this love of the land, this way of life, emanates. I can trace some of the roots, and can account for some of the factors, but the sum is greater than the parts I can name. A ledger can't answer a question going to fundamental values.

What the ledger goes record, however, is a substantial expenditure for planting, for machinery, labor, and conservation expense. The initial cost of the 10,000 seedlings came to $200, but that was only a small part of the outlay. Payments for gas, oil, machinery rental, labor, and overhead came to several times the cost of seedlings. That was for the planting; then came necessary erosion-control work, conservation projects, fire-break and trail work.

Through it all — through the planning, scheduling, cash outlays, and work — there are intangible benefits. We went on a picnic on Pike Bay (off Takagami Loop) last June, in the sand dunes. It was a perfect beach for Tony and David and we lolled in the sun and alternately played in the shallow, gently sloping shore water. Afterwards we went to the south end of the bay, near the public picnic grounds, to look for the ancient Indian portage trail that once cut south through a chain of three little lakes to Leech Lake. There was no trace after generations of logging, fires, and man's compulsion to landscape natural beauty. We found a few pottery shards in the water — probably brought up by heaving ice during spring breakup and then washed ashore. I explained to the boys that the water level was up two feet from the days when the first Americans had exclusive use of the land.

"Why?"

"Because of the dam at the lake outlet."

"Why did they build a dam?"

Why indeed? It did not generate power; logs were no longer floated down the river; it was of minimal use in flood control.

"I can't think of a good reason," I tell them.

Then we headed inland to the site of the deserted experimental forest plots, about three miles east of the bay, which had been laid out during the heyday of the CCC but now had fallen into neglect. One of the plots was overgrown with caragana (Siberian pea). This hardy, thorny bush produces beanlike pods in late summer and fall on which local and migrating birds like to feed. The roots, tenacious as the branches, hold against washouts, and I have found caragana a multi-purpose asset. We dug and pulled fifty little plants, wrapped the roots in wet newspapers, and loaded the lot in a big portage pack for the hike out.

We planted them in a washout gully in the early evening, when it was cool, but still daylight. The gully borders the east field in an eroded area. I returned to the planting with a backpack water tank weighing nearly fifty pounds, and with Tony and David trailing along. When I refilled the tank for a second trip they tried to lift it, then noticed my sweaty face and soaked shirt.

"Do you *have* to do that, Daddy?" Tony tends to be protective of me.

"Yes. Plants need water, especially when you dig them up and replant them. That's a shock for them. The water helps settle the roots, it gets the air out and compacts the earth, and helps to restart the nourishment cycle." More answer than they'd bargained for; Peggy keeps telling me I lecture too much.

The children came along for the second trip, gently tamping in the new plants as I watered them. It pleases me when they do things without having to be asked or told.

There was no ledger entry for the caragana. If one could reduce it to tangible terms, would it be expense or income? Debit or credit? Capital investment? Depreciable? Appreciable.

Tree farm cash outlay for the year had come to nearly $3,000. We should have grossed about $1,000 for Christmas trees and another $1,000 or more for the live-tree sale, plus the $1,500 pulpwood sale we did complete, for a total gross income of $3,500. If one of the two canceled sales had materialized we would have broken even or done a little better. But both failed; we had gambled and lost. Better luck next year, though we'll have to do some hard figuring to determine how much of a planting we can afford.

The money question is weighing on me, intruding on my thoughts. I'd been shoving it away for some months — a recurring conundrum that reappears over the years. Tax time brings it to the fore, making me face up to the needs for a more prudent, objective approach. We'd known all along that the minimum return time of our multigeneration crop would be twenty to thirty years, barring the odd pulpwood sale or returns from culling. That's why we chose diversified tree farming. Of the 200 acres, less than half are in plantations begun on open fields. About 60 acres are in existing natural tree stands, which we tend and harvest with care, and spot-plant or replant as indicated. The remainder of the land is marsh, two lakes of about 5 acres each (though they are over thirty feet deep — cold, spring-fed ponds ringed by deep peat), and the creek which flows between the two lakes and then into the Mississippi.

Income has to come from the periodic cuttings of the natural stand, from thinning of the plantation for Christmas trees or posts and poles, and from landscaping stock from the natural stand. The dilemma is that a planting, of any size, costs. Seedlings come to about 20 percent of the cost; then equipment, gas and oil, labor, travel, insurance mount up (though I do much of the work myself and the family helps as it can). There's nothing for it; I must keep planting and other costs in more reasonable, direct relationship to income — not to expected, anticipated, wished-for, or even contracted-for income, but to bird-in-hand income. We'll have to cut back on our plans for this coming season and delay them until we have the money set aside. I dislike having to put off planting the cedar, and having to lose yet another year before establishing the sugar maple grove.

It's very cold today. Minus-twenty Fahrenheit at daybreak, to barely zero at midday. High snow still, compacting only slightly as result of wind, gravity; and there is insufficient warmth from the sun to give it crust, though there is crystallization. During such weather my first years on the farm I would go out on skis, but I found them clumsy in the brush. I had owned the skis previously, and was used to them as wintertime conveyances. It took me a while to graduate to snowshoes, discovering what Indians had known for a long time: they're quicker, quieter, easier in deep snow and brush. Also, when I'm out in the woods and tired, they make magnificent rests — one on the ground for a seat, the other stuck in the snow for a backrest.

I went for a sortie toward the river, wearing very light clothing and a weatherproof coverall, wool socks, felt shoes, four-buckle overshoes, and a wool cap with ear flaps. I had goggles and a face mask in my pocket, but did not need them. Cotton gloves inside mittens were all right. It was unusually quiet in the woods today, and there were few tracks. The deer must be holed up elsewhere; didn't see a single hoof mark either on high ground or in the marsh. A few bird and partridge tracks, one weasel track (ermine, now that it is winter).

The magic came not only from the silence and the seeming emptiness of the land, but also from the white dusting of frost rime and snow powder on the trees. Every pine needle, every branch was dusted with the confectionary sugar — a sweetening of the world by the breath of winter. Also, the branches hung low over accustomed trails, an illusion caused by the two- to three-foot depth of the snow, which raised me rather than lowered them. Bumping a branch brought a fine sifting of frost and snow, traces on my face and down the collar crevice — not an unpleasant contrast from the body warmth.

I rested near the top of the hill and looked out over the second lake, which was covered with ice over two feet thick, and with a blanket of snow atop the ice. No tracks. There could have been wolf, fox, deer; but the snow was undisturbed. Closer, the woods showed signs of the logging we had done — a branch sticking up here and there, an empty space where tall spruce had stood before. Not quite totally empty: even in deep snow the tops of young spruce were protruding, offspring of the big trees that had had to come down.

One summer night under a full moon I had come up on this same spot. It had been a warm day, but the evening had turned cool quickly, and the night air had brought the chill closer to the marrow. Ground fog had formed, lying close to the earth in low spots, but rising, ballooning, expanding rapidly as I walked through the plantation until visibility was limited to a few feet in any direction and I had to find my way by rote. As I came up the hill I rose above ground-fog level; an instant brought my head through the clouds, so to speak, then the rest of me, and a world tinted silver greeted my view. A magic, surrealistic world different from any I had known, because hilltops, tall trees, and other landmarks rose above the mist like

mountaintops through the clouds, while all the familiar contours — the lakes, the trails, the familiar shapes below — had disappeared.

That experience had never been repeated; nor do I suppose will I ever again see what I saw today when I rose from my hilltop rest and snowshoed the rest of the way to the river. For there the frost rime was even more pronounced, coating the dead reeds and cattails along the riverbanks, and the willows and alders crowding the edge, and the pines on the opposite bank. The river was open — a dark gurgle flowing past icy shores; the black-and-white contrast was made even starker by the static ice and snow on the land and the relentless flow of the water. It was later than I realized; the sun was lowering toward the horizon, still bright and glaring, but changing in tone and shade, until in a matter of minutes it had turned golden and the world around me was golden-hued: the rime, the ice, each branch, pine needle, icicle — all gold. It didn't last long, a few minutes at most, and then the gold dissipated to dusk.

My farm has many colors, even if the green of money is sometimes scarce.

The solitary walk yesterday helped me put the finances in perspective. I've reluctantly canceled planting cedar and maple this year; we'll do it another. Perhaps one or both of the broken sales contracts will come though; if they do, we'll put the money aside as we always do with tree farm income and use it the following spring. It's a setback, but we've had others. We'll spend what time and energy we have on work that doesn't entail dollar investment this spring and summer, like limbing Norway pine, transplanting birch and swamp dogwood, and getting a few more tamarack up from the swamp — they do well on high ground.

Tamarack, or larch, are the only pine to lose their needles in autumn. The green growth turns gold and then cascades into soft heaps around the base of the trees. In the spring the pale green new needles, almost silvery, are among the first new greens to be seen — soft, feathery harbingers of the season that turn a darker, more traditional shade of green as the short needles harden and become tumescent. Tamaracks are thought of as lowland trees, but they thrive upland too. I'm told that they once grew throughout the terrain, but were considered useless and cut during the logging days, left to survive only in the swamps. They also are shade-intolerant and cannot compete with other species. I like them and consider them desirable, especially juxtaposed with the Norway pine that constitute the bulk of the plantation. Right now the tamarack are bare, resting for another season.

Am I a hopeless romantic? Some of my city friends have suggested that removing myself from urban life constitutes escapism. They come to visit, usually during the temperate summer, enjoy the beauties of the country, and want to hear stories of wildlife and natural phenomena. Somehow in the back of their minds they know we work hard, sometimes have to struggle, but it's all so healthy, so "ecological," so romantic. They don't want to hear about weeds or telephones; they want to hear about sunsets and northern lights. Perhaps the escapism is theirs more than mine.

My mind keeps coming back to this in relationship to the answer, if I can find one, to the question of the financial viability of tree farming and the aesthetics of this lifeway. Factored by what? One's values?

Last night's golden sunset is still very real to me, but it does not diminish my acceptance of other equally real and quite different aspects of our life here — like the scrap over the weeds, or the telephone war. Both are as much a part of this place and our life here as are the night the northern lights glowed fiery red or the day the work bee saved the dead neighbor's farm for his family.

Seeds of some of the noxious weeds, such as hoary alyssum, apparently came into the area mixed in regular farm seed during the days before there was inspection for such contamination. Now they are endemic, scattered in the ground throughout the region — all ground, that is, that has been tilled at one time or another or disturbed. Here and there one even finds noxious weeds in the woods, where open space and lack of competition or shading make their growth possible.

Where the land is plowed and cultivated annually, the weeds are usually under some degree of control. But in pastures, field borders, and in plantations there is an outburst of the weeds. After my third year of tree farming, some of the township farmers began to demur at the weeds on my plantation, especially where scalping or furrowing had released the dormant seeds.

"They'll spread to our fields."

"They're already in your fields. The ground's full of them."

"There's a law about controlling weeds. You'll have to spray them. Especially the hoary alyssum."

"The spray'll destroy the trees; the only real control over weeds will come from the trees shading them out; it'll take a few years, but that's permanent weed control. Spraying doesn't work; like the cockle — even 2-4-5-T won't destroy cockle. And no spray will touch the seeds in the ground."

Neither side convinced the other, and the argument came to engulf the township weed commissioner, the county soil conservation organization, Forestry, and before long there was a hornet's nest astir over the issue. I tried hand-pulling weeds and made only a small dent, although the whole family spent many hours in the heat, pulling the rough-stemmed plants.

Finally the county extension forester cast the deciding vote.

"You'll have to spray fifty feet wide along the fences bordering cultivated fields," he ruled. "The manufacturers guarantee the spray won't harm conifers, so long as the directions are followed and you don't spray while the trees are candling."

The spraying devastated the pine trees, which burned, died, or turned to grotesqueries — misshapen, stunted abnormalities. But the weed still thrived, and ultimately we had to plow-under the stunted trees and the few survivors in a belt fifty feet wide and more than half a mile in length. It was a bitter thing and futile, and the stench of herbicide is still like the stink of death in my nostrils. When it was done I swore it would never be repeated, and the empty strip has since been replanted with trees, which have now crowded out the weeds. I also said after the fiasco that if anyone tried to push me into unilateral action to control weeds again, I'd meet them in court — and we'd go after *all* the weeds declared noxious by law — on all contiguous land, or none; I would not be party to a selective action aimed at one species on one plot of land. It was the end of the matter, and a couple of years ago the forester involved, who's since gone on to work elsewhere, met me in the farm store. We talked about this and that, and he finally said:

"Sorry about that weed business; it was a mistake."

"Well, it's over and done." I told him, though, that when I sprayed herbicide I concurrently ran a controlled experiment, putting out flags to mark the different plots. I started out with the mix prescribed by the manufacturer and diluted it progressively by stages. In none of the plots, from first to last, did the herbicide control the weeds; but in all the plots the young trees were burned. I had no choice about the spraying. But while I was at it I thought I might as well prove to myself, and perhaps to others, that it could be harmful. As it turned out, it proved even more damaging than I had suspected, although my way of experimenting lacked the scientific controls and precise measurements that an agricultural research organization would bring to it.

"I didn't know the stuff hurt conifers," he said, and he really did regret what had happened; but in the political equation of the township, there were several score regular farmers and one tree farmer.

"I hear that's the same stuff they used in the defoliation spraying in Vietnam," I said.

"Yup. D'you ever replant the strip?"

"Yes."

"Good."

I'd felt helpless at the time it happened, unable to cope with the various organizations and interest groups with whom I carried little weight no matter how persuasive my arguments might have been. But I could understand where the farmers were coming from; theirs had been a losing effort to cope with weeds that impaired pasture and crops. And while the weeds on my land were no worse than the weeds on theirs, they saw tree farming as frivolous and fruitless.

Time and results have changed things. Some of my

neighbors now see advantage in tree cultivation, over and above shelter belts. The trees control erosion and retain ground moisture, which benefits the water table. And the trees provide cash crop as Christmas trees and later as posts and poles. That sounds good, and it is good, until you have a bad year (Don't I sound like the rest of the farmers, though?)

The telephone business was different. I'd been warned by a fellow living up the road a few miles who had moved into the township a few years before me, one of the first city transplants, that newcomers were likely to be "taken" if they allowed it. "It's not only a game," he cautioned, "like trying out the new kid in school. It's also to see how much juice can be squeezed out of the lemon; if they get some, that's fine. If they don't, well, nothing's lost." I heard him but I didn't listen. For a while.

Then there came a day when I wanted a telephone, after a couple of years of enjoying being without.

"Can't help you," I was told. "Ma Bell doesn't come in here. It's territory preempted by the co-op."

"That's fine. I believe in co-ops. Where do I join?"

"Line's full; we can't take any more."

I met with the eight members who constituted the co-op, and found out that indeed their line preempted the area and had done so since telephone service came in. What's more, the line was in tough shape, the poles leaning every which way and the wires sagging.

"We got to rebuild the line to take you on," the president said. "So if you pay for the rebuilding, you can get a phone."

"How much would that be?"

"Eight thousand dollars." It might as well have been eight million. It didn't take them long to find out I didn't have eight thousand. So the talk shifted to how many others would want to get on. There were quite a few, but the most that could be handled by a rebuilt line would be sixteen phones — the eight old ones and eight new ones. And it was expected that the newcomers would pay the cost of the rebuilding of the whole line for everyone, at a thousand dollars apiece.

"Nobody's got that kind of money," I said, "and besides, it isn't fair."

Well, we were at a standstill. They wouldn't budge and I couldn't pay. And there matters would have stayed had the president not felt compelled to add: "If you want it bad enough, you'll have to pay for it. We did."

That did it. "I'm willing to pay my share, but not yours. And I'm willing to put in my work, like everybody else. But I'm not willing to be taken advantage of or to be pushed around. Now what's it going to be? Are we going share and share alike? Or work out a formula for old and new members?"

"Newcomers pay for the whole thing," he said. "That's final."

"You can take that Toonerville Trolley line of yours and . . ." Somebody was pulling on my sleeve by then. I was angry and showing it. I took another, calmer approach. "You're discriminating against the people who want phones and who need them, and there are more than eight, or sixteen, in this township who fall in that category. And there's a remedy for that."

I guess we weren't steeped in love that night, any of us, and not for a while after. I went to the large parent telephone co-op to find out if they would help if we lined up a substantial number of new customers, but they had to turn us down for a number of reasons. Ma Bell said yes indeedy, they'd love to provide the service and could do it handsomely, with newfangled cables and Princess phones and extensions and the like, *but* . . . the territory was preempted.

I canvassed the township and signed up over thirty families that did not have phones and wanted them, then appealed to the Minnesota Public Service Commission, which called a public hearing. It lasted all day. We all suffered in white shirts and ties, except for the attorney hired by the co-op, who was used to this way of dressing. It hadn't occurred to me or to the others who wanted phones to hire a lawyer, but we didn't have the money for it even if we had thought of it.

The proceedings got a little rough, but acting as attorney in our behalf I guess I gave as good as we got, or maybe a little better. We had photos of the Toonerville Trolley line, as it came to be called, showing the leaning poles propped by makeshift supports, and we had proof of refusal of service, and refusal to share costs. When the ruling finally was issued some weeks later, precedent was set which allowed two telephone companies to operate in the same territory. We thirty got ours from Ma Bell, and the eight co-op members continued their operation. But before the year was out they dismantled the old line and switched to Ma Bell. I had very mixed feelings about that because I really would have preferred the co-op way. It was a convenience to have the phone (and a couple of times has been a lifesaver, as during fires and accidents), the more so for the older and isolated people who had been going without. Even here in the north woods we've come to prefer "paying for it" to "doing for it." And damn it, I still would have preferred cooperating and rebuilding — but it takes a willingness to do it by all involved.

I played piano last night, practicing Chopin Etudes nos. 6 and 7; they're not popular and are rarely performed, but I like the musicality that emerges when the technical difficulties have come under control. I really should try to get a chamber-music group together. I have been saying that for several years and somehow have never done anything about it.

Piano playing distracts my conscious mind. I concentrate, seeking to satisfy the pitch and expression that my inner ear requires of me. My technical skills usually fall short of my private standards of acceptable musicianship, and I don't play for others. But the process compels me to concentrate and some of the music seeps into my subconscious, to say there whatever it is it has to say.

This reminds me of an old acquaintance, John Laubin, who lives in Wyoming, in even greater winter isolation than I do. John and his wife are accomplished artists and dancers who have performed internationally. For many years their speciality has been to research and validate Indian dances and rituals on the verge of extinction. They still do field work and perform in the summer, and do their writing and research in the winter. They live in a cabin at the foot of the Tetons and occasionally are snowed in. John is a fair violinist and obtains Minus One recordings of chamber music and concerti. When the snow piles up, he sits by the huge picture windows looking out upon the Tetons' peaks, puts on the records, and plays solo violin concerti with the world's greatest orchestras. We each find our ways; I admire his.

It's still cold; there has been no break in the weather pattern. But the deer are back. I came home late tonight after playing Scrabble with W.H. in town. About a mile north of the homestead in the snow-covered pasture across from the Hansen's farmstead there were seventeen deer coming from the tamarack swamp and heading northwest. They're probably in my woods now, if they didn't keep going. Snow depth is borderline for them to move around in. Any more snow now and they'll begin to yard up, which could mean trouble for them. Once they trample a yard and there is even more snow, they can get trapped in there and starve. We'll have to be watchful, arrange to feed them if necessary.

There are sun dogs, looking like three little sunlets on each side of the real thing. A total of six atmospheric illusions. Shimmering. Pale gold in whitish blue sky. A sign of great cold and more to come.

What a cold spell it's been. Forty-five below most nights, never warmer than minus-ten at midday. I live in my heavy wool socks; the felt boots and overshoes are by the door. While it's a temptation to wear the felt boots in the house as well, cozying in their warmth and softness, I've found that the perspiration accumulates, and once outdoors my feet get colder more quickly. They are still very sensitive after frostbite years ago.

"How did you get frostbite, Daddy?"

"I was careless," I tell Tony, not feeling like talking about it.

"Does it still hurt?" David persists, literal as always.

"No, only when my feet get very cold. Now how about it, shall we go outside and do some work?"

"In this weather?" Everyone seems dubious about going out in the cold. "Doing what?"

"Those brush piles we made in the cutover and planned to burn down. Let's go cut some of them for firewood."

Nobody rushes to get dressed; nor does anybody overwhelm me with offers of assistance.

"We can have a winter picnic out there, and bring a skidload of wood back for a big fire tonight." Not that we lack firewood at the house, though we are conscious of the need to keep the woodpile up.

"It's warmer today, ten above." It isn't much, but it is a little bit of an inducement. "And we can have angels-on-horseback." That gets to the kids: roasted marshmallows between two pieces of chocolate bar, with graham crackers on the outsides. (Our dentist thrives on them.)

So we troop outside and work in the cold, not feeling it due to our exertion. We have a lively fire going in the snow, more for the spirit of it than for actual warmth, and after sawing up bigger pieces of brush not completely buried by the snow and stacking them on the tobogganlike skid, we make the angels-on-horseback. It is cold, now that we are standing still, but not unbearably so. In ten-degree weather on a windless day I've more than once worked in shirtsleeves.

"I like this better than burning down the brush pile," I say, looking at the skidload of middle-sized sticks.

My wife nods. "It makes more sense."

I know what she means; it shows more respect for the wood, as much of a resource and a product of the farm as any other harvest.

We head home pulling the ropes, with the children pushing more or less regularly. And it falls into place in my mind a little better, as I tug and pull during the half-mile trip. While I can't put the equation in algebraic terms, I know that the factor I have been seeking is not only our values, but also a matter of respect. You have to respect nature and wildlife in order to savor what they have to offer; you have to respect other people before you can love them or partake of their proffer, and you have to respect yourself. You have to respect your neighbors, who and what they are, and hope to obtain their respect in reciprocity. And when that doesn't happen you have to dig in your heels. So whether it's golden sunsets or weeds or telephones or silvery woods in midwinter, respect is a factor in the equation along with your values.

And the money? Well, I guess you have to respect that too to the extent that when you have it, you put it aside to plant trees next year.

11

Fire

I T IS THE FIRE SEASON. Last year in April there was a huge forest fire in Canada at least a hundred miles north of us. Haze and ash were in the air for days; sunlight was filtered to sulphurous ochre creating a prolonged eclipse. We could only guess at the devastation.

I am in town shopping for bulk grease and hardware items after lunch when heavy smoke begins rising in the skies. Momentary fear that it is the farm. But the farm is east of town, just below the first southward bend of the Mississippi, and the plume is farther north. The smoke does not abate, stays at the same intensity several minutes, then becomes darker, larger, rising up higher in a column and spreading more quickly. This signals more heat, more combustion. It looks to be two, perhaps three miles away.

My heavy clothing and boots are already in the trunk of the car; so are shovel, axe, and other tools.

That's as automatic as is the presence of the winter kit from November through March, when the trunk holds my packed suitcase containing a complete outfit of warm clothing, matches, boots, and sleeping bag, in case of car breakdown or accident in sub-zero weather. In spring and fall, when dead grass mats the landscape and the fire hazard is extreme, the winter kit is exchanged for fire-fighting paraphernalia. The tradition here is that whoever can help, does so. In extreme circumstances passersby can be stopped and pressed into fire-fighting service.

According to my car radio, what started as an out of control grass fire has jumped into the woods and is spreading rapidly. I know the area. Heavily forested with jack pine and Norway, most of it planted by CCC in the 1930's on tax-forfeited lands taken over by state or county. After the country was logged-over at the turn of the century, and through the 1920's, there had been no replanting. The accumulated slash fed forest fires during the dry periods, and the fires raged over the land. Not until the New Deal years did there come to be extensive reforestation. The young men who made up the Civilian Conservation Corps of the Depression years changed the denuded landscape of our country for the better and to the benefit of countless generations. Now one of these plantations is burning. The smoke is heavier, rising high in a vertical column, blowing northward at almost a right angle after reaching a height of two hundred feet.

I pass the State Forestry ranger headquarters on my way out of town and notice that it is deserted, the motor pool empty. The arrow on the multicolored fire danger index is pointing to red: extreme danger. Well it might. The land is dry, the snow is gone, the new growth has not started. There is no natural barrier to the fire. How far north does the forest reach before water, rock, or other natural obstacle would stop a fire? There are some scattered little lakes ten miles away, but they are encircled by woods and present no barrier. Farther north and west are Upper and Lower Red Lake, but the wind direction will drive the fire east of these huge expanses of water. Roads and highways are no barrier to a large fire, and this one could go for great distances. The first natural barrier is a hundred miles away at the Canadian border, where rock and rivers stop the woods . . . Impossible. I'm letting my imagination feed my fears — adding fuel to the empathy a tree farmer feels for the forest rangers.

On the road north I draw nearer to the smoke. The blacktopped highway is sprinkled with ash, although the wind is blowing the smoke away to the north and I am approaching from the south. So there must already be back eddies of wind, invisible whorls of air spewing around like miniature cyclones. The air is acrid with smoke — pungent, hot.

It must have started half a mile or more to my right. I can see smoldering grass, wisps of ochre smoke in the hayfield there. A little farther along is a broadening wedge of blackened, still-smoldering grassland and up ahead now rolling clouds of smoke and the first sighting of flaming trees, where field meets forest. Most trees are charred sticks, flame licking here and there.

The fire is still farther ahead. No people in sight, but three cars and a pickup truck are parked on the shoulder of the road; a dump truck with flatbed trailer attached is off in the ditch. Have they gotten a bulldozer out here this quickly to plow a fire line?

Up ahead smoke billows over the road, obscuring the view. Should I drive through? It is sheeting over the highway in gusts now. Walls of flame have been known to flare out, and I consider the risks. The highway is wide, it has shoulders and then ditches on both sides, and the woods don't start for another fifteen to twenty feet beyond. Total width of clear area must be between eighty and a hundred feet, and the forest on my left, to the west, is as yet untouched. I decide to take the chance, roll up the car windows while driving closer, take a deep breath, and step on the accelerator. Through the smoke, a moment's sensation of heat, and then I'm safe, but in the fire zone.

It is a sinister landscape cast in an ominous half-light, because the sky overhead is a racing, rolling, roiled and scudding curtain of black smoke. It is a half-night raining ash and carbon particles. The only stars are burning embers. The sun is wearing a shroud and the hopes of foresters and all who love growing things are ashes.

The fire is burning parallel to the highway but still a quarter mile in. Ahead I can see a collection of vehicles, figures in motion. A fire line is working from a sandy crossroad. There are men with backpacks of water — heavy canisters weighing seventy pounds and more. Others with chain saws, axes, shovels, brush hooks. But as I prepare to get out of the car there is shouting. I hear whistle blasts from down the sand road.

"Everybody out and up to the next crossroad. Quarter mile up the highway."

Evidently the fire cannot be held here and is about to jump, or has already jumped the fire line. Mad scramble into cars and trucks. Somebody waves a Bemidji fire department tanker truck, just arriving, to keep going.

We all park facing north, on both shoulders of the highway, in case this fire line doesn't hold either. The ranger in command is Frank Hubbard, a craggy-faced, sturdy man in his fifties wearing a Stetson. He shouts at the disembarking men: "Water on the right. Wet it down. This crew, *you*, clear brush and debris on the left. At least thirty feet back from the road. You over there, take your crew on the left. All trees and brush down. Thirty feet wide." He is trying to widen the new fire line north from the sandy crossroad, and meanwhile slow down the oncoming fire.

Frank runs down the sandy road in a rolling gait, sniffing smoky air, glancing up at the violently swirling smoke overhead to gauge the speed and intensity of the fire. I'm right behind him as he jerks to a halt, turns to the crews strung out along the sand road. They are slower, carrying backpacks and gear, running as best they can after refilling water packs from the tanker.

"Come on," Frank yells. "It'll be coming out about here. From here on down. Hey, you back there! Don't waste time and water down there. Come on, here!"

Frank and I know each other casually. He turns to me: "I need more men. We should be cutting trees before the fire crowns. Go back up to the corner and send anybody you can find. Axes, saws, anything."

I run back, wheezing and coughing from the bad air, and realize that I was about a quarter of a mile in from the highway. More cars and trucks are pulling up. A Chippewa National Forest truck from Cass Lake, seventeen miles from the fire site, is disgorging the fire-fighting crew from Cass Lake High School, one of the best crews around. They are tough young men, Indian and non-Indian, who vie for places on the crew and are on standby during the fire seasons. A special school bell summons them when the rangers ask for their help. The bell brings them running from their classes; their fire-fighting clothes are stored in school lockers, and the youths race to the forestry truck waiting in front of the school, changing en route. The crew is paid on an hourly basis, and only a little above the minimum wage, but they are woods-wise and know what they are doing.

I send all new arrivals down the road and watch Frank put them to work trying to stem the oncoming fire and widen the fire line. There is no point of eleva-tion from which the fire can be seen, and Frank and the other rangers have to go by the sound, smell, and smoke to determine how fast it is approaching, how intensely it is burning, whether the trees are being charred by the quick-burning underbrush and grass, or whether the heat is intense enough for the trees themselves to burn. Eventually such a fire crowns, with the most intense heat and balls of fire rolling through tree-tops in advance of the flames on the ground. Such a crown fire can move with tremendous speed. The crown fire can leap, jump, skip — and make the advance of a ground fire seem to happen at a snail's pace.

The tanker truck is already empty and heading back to town for a refill; there are no streams or potholes to pump from. The backpack crews have been straggling out to the corner for refills and then returning to the fire front: it is not safe for vehicles to come down the sandy crossroad that constitutes our fire line. Is it safe for us? The men are sweaty, red-faced from heat, coughing. Everyone's eyes are red, watering.

Though we are too close to gauge the full dimension of the fire, we see that the smoke is growing thicker, blacker; the area of fire larger; there is even less daylight. The fire front is widening, creeping closer to the highway on the west, and heaven knows how far to the east, where there are no roads. Whatever the extent and speed of the spread to the sides, the fastest advance is northward, toward us, for it is driven by the unrelenting wind from the south. There are first signs now that the fire is engendering its own winds — that the rapidly released heat and gases are making their own storms. God forbid it becomes a fire storm! It is growing so fast!

The first outcroppings of flame reach the fire line, stop momentarily, then leap in little bursts as clumps of grass, brush, trees flare up forty, fifty, sixty feet ahead of the advancing wall of flame which crackles

toward us. Boys and men run and jump to douse the little outbursts torched by heat and sparks, but Frank calls the fire line off. Another retreat — thousands more trees sacrificed so that an even greater number might be saved.

"Next crossroad up. Come on, hurry. Next road up." It's another quarter mile and Frank makes sure the last men down the line have heard. Then he hurries out and the fire roars and belches where we had stood and fought.

The cars and trucks move helter-skelter. Frank has more rangers now from other stations, and he can give them orders to relay to crew leaders and to crews. Mapping the next stand, he drives up the highway. The walkie-talkies are not much use in this heat, and Frank talks personally to the leaders, then takes up his stand at the corner of the highway and a new sand-road fire line. Over a hundred men are fire fighting now; more are arriving, as are sightseers.

Frank uses his car radio to check with the ranger station dispatcher. Loud static, but an intermittent voice responds.

"Where's the spotter plane?" Frank asks.

". . . heat . . . driven off . . ."

Frank spits, licks his lips. "Where's the bulldozer?"

So there *is* a bulldozer out there on the east side — trying to hem the fire in, trying to push it into a narrower channel, pinching it between its broad, traveling scalp and the highway where we are.

". . . don't know . . . wait . . ."

Suddenly the dispatcher's voice booms loud and

clear: "Pilot sees the dozers. Three of them. They got a good wide strip going, but they can't head it in much, and it keeps getting ahead of them."

"At least it isn't getting any wider over there," Frank says to himself. Back into the radio: "Thanks. I got no contact with those dozers. Can't reach them. If they get in trouble there's no way I can get over there."

"We gotcha," the dispatcher replies. "We'll try and watch them. Pilot says it's crowning and the updrafts forced him to back off."

"Tell me something I don't know," Frank snarls, and hangs up the microphone.

He leaves supervision of the fire line to a subordinate. Small crews have to be placed along the highway now to keep the fire from jumping across. A couple of small spot fires have already started and could lead to disaster; if it takes off on the other side of the blacktop the fire could trap us.

I've been too busy working on the line or running errands for Frank, who uses me because the rangers are more use as fire-line supervisors. I notice the sightseers now: some mothers who have picked up children from school and cannot or dare not drive farther; motorists using the highway and caught by the smoke and the fire. I see the figure of the aging Clem Oberberg, the county land commissioner who is far past retirement age but who is so wrapped up in his lifelong work of land acquisition and reforestation he does not retire. Much of this forest is Clem's work, and I'm shocked to see him here witnessing its destruction. I fear that the pain of seeing this can be too much for him to bear. The work of his life has been one of passionate, almost monomaniacal devotion: acquiring this land as a public holding and reforesting it, then managing it on a sustained-yield basis and using the profits to help finance the schools. He saw to that, this son of immigrant German freethinkers. Now Oberberg is waddling up rapidly on his bent, spindly legs. He is red-faced, red-eyed, sweating and panting, and he all but clutches Frank's lapels.

"It's burning almost to the road, Frank." Oberberg is on the verge of hysteria. "Please, Frank, help me save the little plantation. The Norways down a piece. Please, Frank, the little Norways!"

The plantation is less than twenty acres of five-year-old trees along the road — a six- or seven-foot high island amid the taller, scragglier, brushier jack pine. Oberberg had supervised their planting as he often did, though such projects were the work of the foresters and Clem was out of his jurisdiction. But the foresters had not minded; everybody respected Oberberg's devotion and commitment.

The fire is already to the highway, burning rapidly through the jack pine and within minutes of devouring the Norway plantation. I know that Frank cannot spare the men. It would take one crew of backpackers and another with shovels to beat back the fire from the plantation — if they could — at the cost of a more rapid advance of the overall fire front. But Frank doesn't blink, doesn't argue. He just looks closely at Oberberg for a moment and then orders the men to save the plantation.

"Just the plantation," he orders. "Nothing else. As soon as you've done that, I need you." He doesn't say: "if you can."

There's distress for everyone — not just for Oberberg; not just for Frank, worried about the cut-off bulldozer crews and the spotter pilot; not just for the men coping with the physical discomforts and the exertion and the constant danger of being burned, or injured by falling branches or trees, or trapped. There's the distress all of us perceive — but especially that of the children in the stalled cars — as singed and burning animals pop out of the woods. A burning porcupine struggles into the ditch, collapses, dies; faster-moving deer and fox come leaping out occasionally, unexpectedly, at times darting between two fire fighters who see and smell the singed and burning fur. The birds have been either overcome or have flown away. The children are open-mouthed, silent, big-eyed.

Ordinarily animals escape a forest fire. They outrun it, fly away, or burrow beneath the surface. But animals are no more immune to the vagaries of wind and to just plain bad luck than humans are. Fires become more capricious as they grow in size. They leapfrog, jump, and skip, especially as a fire crowns and races ahead at the treetops faster than the slower-burning ground fire. Smoke blinds and confuses animals as it does men, and burning branches and trees fall on them. Fire fighters are sometimes trapped, singed, burned, or suffocated; so are animals in the wild. And this fire is taking a toll of wildlife.

I work with the crews in the plantation. It is a mat-

ter of beating back the flames with water from backpacks, squirted through hand-held hoses with pump
levers; and of beating back flames with shovels or
other tools. Each of us is face-to-face with flames, heat,
and a small slice of battlefield. We don't know how the
others are doing. We each beat, smash, pound at the
flames in front of us, popping up at our sides, behind
us; as the fire leaps, dances, cavorts around us, we dart
from tree to tree at the plantation boundary. Then the
fire passes the start of the plantation, and we fight at
the sides — running, jumping, leaping, beating. Breath
comes short, sweat dries up, skin feels as though it is
cracking where not covered by clothing.

Most of the plantation is saved — an island of green
in a black landscape. But the fire has eaten its way to
the highway with full force above and below us, as
though to make up for being pushed back from its
rightful prey at the plantation. It burns with renewed
intensity, furor. As we stagger out to the highway we
see a small fenced plot in the way of the flames. It is an
old, overgrown township cemetery — the tombstones
weathered and stained, grass and weeds attesting its
unkempt neglect. An old pioneer cemetery, repository
of long-ago pursuers of dreams. Some of us instinc-
tively move to save the cemetery from being engulfed,
but they remember what Frank had said: "Only the
plantation. I need you." Life and living things need us
more than the dead. We trot, jog, up the road to meet
Frank — and it pains me; pains all of us, I suspect.

The crews are sent to join a newly established fire
line on yet another sandy crossroad. We have retreated

half a mile this time. Then Frank siphons off several crews to leapfrog the new line. He takes them another half mile farther north, to the next crossroad, and directs them: "Lay it all down. Everything. As far back as you can. Pile it up big near the corner. They're fighting to give us time down there. Now use it."

A backfire! He's getting ready to set a backfire. Over half a mile south of us the fire roars on — ever bigger, higher, flames beginning to tower in columns. I hope the fire line can hold it long enough for us to cut a wide strip and backfire. The chain saws roar and spew chips; men without saws drag branches, logs, and stumps into the woods and toward the oncoming fire. It's still too far away to be heard except as a faint roar, but the smoke and ash are suffusing the air.

I know the idea of a backfire is to eliminate the fuel from the path of an oncoming fire and thereby stop it. Also I've heard that if done right, the two fires — backfire and oncoming fire — can be made to burn each other out, like using dynamite to blast out an oil-well fire by taking away the oxygen. But I've never seen this done.

"Go down there and get me the Cass Lakers and the tanker truck," Frank tells me. I hand off my saw and run for the car, turn it around, and head back. Heavy smoke is billowing across the highway and I see figures fighting spot fires darting in and out of the trees on the west side. The tanker has gone again for another refill.

"Frank wants it up at the backfire," I tell the ranger in charge.

"They said they weren't coming back. Highway isn't safe anymore."

"Well, send the Cass Lakers up there, Frank says," I relay. He says he will and I run for the car again, then drive south through the heavy smoke, wondering what kind of fool I am to be taking such chances. Suddenly next to the car there is flame amid the smoke — a ball of yellow. Then I am in the clear, driving through charred and burned-over country. The skin on my left hand and the left side of my face feels hot and dry; then I am beyond the start of the fire and in clean air and clear light for the first time in hours, making the sudden transition from half-light, half-night of the fire front to the normal world, and for a moment I can't believe that it is daylight and clear and clean somewhere in this world.

At the outskirts tavern, the nearest phone, I call the fire station. "What do you mean it's risky?" I yell. "I just drove through to call you. Yeah, sure, a piece of cake. If my car can make it, so can you. Okay, they want it four miles north of the junction." I realize as I say it that the fire has already gone three miles farther, and I'm amazed at my audacity in ordering the fire department around and in lying so glibly. (And lie I do, because I have second-degree burns on my hand and cheek.)

A portly salesman, sitting at the bar, says: "I hear there's a fire. They should order planes in to drop water bombs — that's what they should do. Call the Air Force over at Duluth and order planes to drop water bombs."

"You're right," I tell him. "Call them and arrange it." When I leave he is still sitting at the bar telling the bartender that water bombs are a good way to fight forest fires.

I get back without incident, no longer intimidated by the smoke, but watchful for fireballs. In passing I see that the fire line is about to be pulled out; the inferno is coming closer and is no longer stoppable. They've slowed it and held it as long as they could, and they would soon be spreading along the highway, some of them joining us at the backfire line.

But where is the backfire? There should be rising smoke half a mile up, but there isn't a wisp.

Again I park on the highway shoulder, facing north in case of another retreat. A small bulldozer has arrived during my absence. It belongs to a farmer a few miles up the highway, and is not one of the lost or separated bulldozers to our east. It has been off-loaded so hurriedly that the trailer and pickup truck used to transport it are still parked in the ditch at an awkward angle. If we have to retreat from here, they might not get the dozer and the truck out. The Cass Lake crew is sprawled on the ground, resting; their water packs are jumbled in the grass. Other crews are down the sandy crossroad with the dozer, pushing back the forest with chain saws, widening and lengthening the firebreak, which now stretches for over half a mile. It needs to be farther yet because the fire front is wider, and they work frantically. Frank stands alone at the corner of crossroad and highway — a cluster of unlit fuses in his hands — staring silently at the small mountain of trees

and brush piled up at the corner marking the beginning of the wide belt that has been cut and piled up,
the beginning of the backfire line; if only he would
light it. He looks stern, unyielding, tense; he glances
down the fire line to gauge progress, then down the
highway at the onrolling clouds of smoke. But most
often, like all of us, he looks up at the sky, because it's a
holocaust that's approaching us — a wall of fire tower-
ing in the sky that roars like an express train, drowning
out all sound but shouts.

I fell like screaming, yelling at Frank to light the
backfire, to do something, anything; but he stands
there as though frozen, occasionally turning his head
one way or the other, and then looking up. He's par-
alyzed; my mind rebels — I must do something, grab
the fuses, light the fire. The wall of fire is over a hundred feet high, less than a quarter mile away, maybe
only an eighth. And the wind has become a storm;
there is no sky, only a blackness overhead. It no longer
rains soot and ash because the storm overhead is carrying it far beyond us.

While my mind has been fighting fear, Frank has lit
the backfire, and I didn't see him do it. So small! A tiny
little fire — a hearth in hell. He looks at it a moment,
lights another fuse, and pitches the pitifully small
Roman candle into the twenty-foot-high pile of brush.
It's like tossing a kitchen match into a blast furnace, I
think. I expect him to begin racing down the firebreak,
throwing more fuses into the woods and starting the
backfire on a broader front, but he stands still at his

corner post, taciturn and unspeaking, contemplating his little blaze.

Without having been told, the Cass Lakers have come to life and have shouldered their water tanks. They saunter down the crossroad, spreading out at intervals, preparing to wet down spot fires on the north side of the sand road. The other men are still far away, lengthening the firebreak, widening it; their chain saws are spewing wood chips in seeming silence, because the roar of the fire obliterates all sound.

The backfire explodes! It crowns in seconds, races to the sky; its own roaring, belching, crackling drowns out the sound of the oncoming disaster. The updraft of the main fire catches the smoke and heat of our backfire blaze, sucks it up, embraces it. The little backfire has become a wall of flame that rushes, speeds away from us at an incredible rate, leaving behind slowly burning char. The backfire races along the firebreak and a quarter mile away it burns up and then away to the south, toward the main blaze. In less than five minutes the backfire has become as large, as fierce and devouring, as the enemy before us.

Flame rises high into the sky; the two fires meet, embrace, conjoin, and convolute. A gigantic explosion and boom as the fires mate. A fiery tower rises high into the sky, then disappears, and we are left with charred and burning trees. The two infernos have engulfed each other: the cannibals have consumed each other. We now have only a fire to fight.

The fire fighters below us have been coming up during this time; I had not noticed. Some are spread along the highway, fighting jump fires on the other side. Under ordinary circumstances some of these jumpers would be sizeable fires. But today there is a different scale of values, of dangers and of threats, and these fires are just jumpers. Tenacious, with a pernicious will and desire of their own, they die stubbornly. Across the firebreak from where the backfire began, other jumpers are engendered by heat and sparks. Crews are dispatched as far as a mile north, fanning out through the forest. Each jumper has potential to start the war anew — a war that could last through the night, the next day, or for days to come.

There is a roar of machines as they come toward us down along the firebreak. The first of three bulldozers comes through, vanguard of the tiny group that hemmed the fire parallel to the highway, edged it in, narrowed it, and at the critical moment met the chain saws of our firebreak crews and kept the fire from turning the flank. The machine's yellow paint is blistered, blackened.

"You all right?" Frank tersely asks the driver, a beefy man in his thirties with crew-cut light brown hair and blue eyes. His face is smudged; there are red patches on his cheeks and hands.

"Some burns, but they ain't bad," he says.

"The others?" Frank inquires.

"They're all right too."

Then Frank smiles, for the first time during the afternoon, and says, "Good job."

It is many hours of grueling work to finish off the fire and its countless offspring; the crews are like Jason seeking to lop off the never-ending growth of new heads, as dragon-teeth seeds of fire sprout. At one point I notice Clem Oberberg sitting by the roadside ditch, resting. He is exhausted, spent, heartbroken. Frank is saying to him: "Look, Clem, we saved the most of it. We'll replant it. We'll plant Norway where the jack pine was. And we did save the little plantation."

Oberberg just nods and doesn't speak. It is hard to be an old man and see a lifelong investment in betterment destroyed. He's probably thinking of the loss of school revenues because of the setback, and that he won't live to see the replanted groves.

The saved little plantation is an anomaly: an incongruous patch of green in a world of black, of charcoal and ashes — a bawling baby amid thousands of mutilated dead and battlefield debris. The tiny roadside cemetery has been totally burned over. The tombstones are blackened and cracked, the fence posts have been incinerated, the fencing is twisted and curled. The land looks as dead as the long-ago people buried here; it is now evident that there have been no funerals conducted here in recent years.

Now I know how Russia looked during the days of World War II. Black earth to stop the Nazi invasion, to delay their advance so that Russia might mobilize and arm and survive. What a terrible, incalculable cost — to incandesce your homeland in a backfire so that the nation might live, just as Frank had set torch to the forest today so that the country for miles around might survive.

The fire has ended — half-night giving way to mustard-colored haze; the air sulphurous, acrid. I drive home to my haven — my tree farm spared from this agony. It was not in danger but I am nonetheless emotionally spent. The burned-over landscape I traverse is a ghostly, worse-than-hell frieze of lifelessness. I cannot bear to describe it. Even leaving it behind me and reentering the world and life, I am numbed, my sensibilities cauterized. Perhaps tomorrow, or another day I will be able to put it all in perspective.

My throat and lungs feel raw; my skin feels parched and burning. The taste of ash is in my mouth though there is none in the air of my tree farm.

"A fire does some good," Peggy tries to reassure me. "It makes minerals available to the soil. It clears away dead grass and second-rate growth. Seeds in the ground can germinate and send out growth free of competition. Or the ground can be planted with profitable trees instead of brush and jack pine."

I know all this but am still too numb to respond to logic. Indians often burn in the spring, a symbolic ritual and a housecleaning, so to speak, as well as a preparation of the soil for planting. Many people still burn off every spring when the frost is in the ground and remnants of snow among the trees, but the dry grass is exposed. It's a relatively safe time to do it. The burning also prevents fires later on when the frost is out and everything is dry, but the greening has not yet started. I have often stood in the pungent smoke (which is traditional in some villages and families), drinking in the smell of burning grass like a narcotic harbinger of spring.

But I'm not ready to be assuaged; the burning of the plantation is not analogous to the annual clearing of the dead grass or to the controlled burning done by foresters as fire prevention or as site preparation for planting.

"Fire is as much a part of nature as ice or snow or a storm," she says. This time she gets to me. And typically, having accomplished her purposes, she changes the subject.

"Did you notice that the ice went out yesterday?"

I'd been so preoccupied that for the first time I'd failed to notice the annual event. The five-month-old ice pan had disintegrated, and now the ducks and loons would return. And in a very Indian way Peggy had brought me out of the depression and dismay and had helped me to see the fire as part of life and nature, as part of the panorama and the yeasting.

It is five years later. We are blueberry picking in the old northern-township burn, finding lots of good berries — as there usually are where there's been a fire. The replanted trees are doing well; all are Norway pine. Some are already showing above the windrows of charred sticks, stumps, and slash. The old pioneer cemetery has been fixed up, fenced, tombstones cleaned and repaired; I wonder who did that. Oberberg? It'd be like him. They say he's going to retire next year, but I don't believe it.

12

Pruning

IT IS BEYOND MY comprehension that we can't get the pruning done. It is fifteen years now and entails trimming the lower branches from two to three hundred large Norway pine, to a height of sixteen feet. It isn't all that hard. And it's desirable. All good texts list the practice near the top in their sections on timber-stand improvement, along with elimination of competing species, brush, and damaged or diseased trees. The pruning has to be done flush to the trunk, and cleanly. It eventually produces lumber clear of knots; it is a fire-safety factor, et cetera. Judicious pruning is like being for motherhood and against sin. We are all agreed on it. Why isn't it getting done?

Tonight I have determined to look into this question scientifically, methodically. To analyze the problem, to be objective, and to find a solution. I leaf through old journals, looking for entries referring to pruning. The first occurs in 1959.

Aug. 30 — Warm, clear. Smith, Paul, and Derek to prune east edge of first hill. Norways there are 135 years old. Forester says should be pruned to produce clear lumber. Use curved pruning saw about nine inches long fastened to long, lightweight aluminum pole.

I'm working on kitchen cabinets when there is a knock on the door. I wish our dog had watchdog instincts or would at least bark. I'm continually surprised by unexpected arrivals whose cars I don't hear because of the noise of hammering and sawing. This time it's a stranger, a huge man who seems to fill the doorway with his bulk, and he is livid. His wife and another couple are in the car, listening through open windows.

"You Mr. Treuer?" He mispronounces it "True-err."

"Yes."

"You keep your brats to keep their clothes on or I'll beat the tar outen them!"

"What are you talking about?"

"If they run around nekkid in front of my wife and folks again that's what I'll do!"

I want to say, "Do what — run around 'nekkid'?" But I think better of it, impressed by his size and considering it wiser to jolly him out of his wrath. So I say, "Just where did this happen?"

"Over on Swenson Lake. A few minutes ago. And I mean to report it to the sheriff, too."

"Those boys are across the road pruning trees." I say it firmly, hoping it is true, but beginning to doubt it.

"The hell they are. And if you're gonna lie about it covering up for them . . ."

The conversation deteriorates, but he is finally persuaded to leave — without being assuaged. I walk through the yard, across the road. Tools lying in the path; no boys. They appear an hour later, claiming to have accomplished a little.

The explanation: a carload of friends who drove by as the boys were starting work invited them to go swimming and they accepted. The fish were biting not far from the usual swimming place, and the two complaining couples were fishing about forty feet out from shore. None of the boys had swimming suits, so they debated, waited, but finally stripped off their clothes and went swimming in the buff.

"Is that all?" It isn't the whole story (which it takes time to elicit). I still don't know if I have it all. Apparently the fishermen were displeased and said so; the boys retaliated by swimming under the boat and tugging on the fishing lines, managing to snarl two together. The fishermen progressed from irritation to anger. The boys responded by coming out of the water and performing pantomimes.

"What kind of pantomimes?" I ask. "Never mind, I don't want to know." They must have been graphic to produce such livid fury.

We'll prune tomorrow.

Sept. 21 — Early supper. We will all go pruning for a couple of hours afterwards. A carload of youngsters pulls into the yard; fifteen humans emerge, including two from the neighboring farm. (Amazing capacity for one dilapidated car.)

"Can your boys play?" someone asks me.

I struggle between the desire to get the pruning job done and the desire to allow the boys opportunity for a little fun. I hear my wife clearly though she isn't saying a word: we live out in the country and they don't have many friends; they need to get acquainted; they shouldn't have to work all the time. Etc.

"Okay, you can play. But tomorrow it's pruning for sure."

They organize a game of kick-the-can; I trudge off with the pruning saw, feeling grouchy . . .

Just beginning to saw the first branch when yells, screams re-call me. One of the bigger visitors had kicked the can simultaneously with twelve-year-old Derek, who is slim and frail. The visitor had missed the can and connected with Derek. Result: broken and dislocated ankle.

We have no phone, so we splint Derek's ankle as best we can, rush him twelve miles to the hospital. Meanwhile visitors drive to nearest phone, alert the doctor, who meets us at the hospital door. Hypo for Derek in the car; then to the emergency room. It's a very bad break, but he should be able to recover without permanent damage.

Oct. 15 — We will prune first hill after school bus picks up boys. My father-in-law pulls in right behind the school bus, announcing that partridge are thick along the old logging road south of Richardson Township School, fifteen miles away. His beloved .410 has just been fixed and he's anxious to try it. We might also get some rabbits over there, and I do love rabbits. Just for the morning . . .

It's a nice day; luck is good. Three birds apiece. We decide to stay a while longer, separate. We meet at the car two hours later. I have three more; Dad has two, and four huge rabbits.

"Thought you'd like them." He's proud. "Snowshoes — big ones. The fur's turned white already."

"Early to be white." I examine the rabbits, glad to get them, then ask, "Just where were they?"

He describes the area, an open patch about a quarter mile away. I calculate mentally, trying to remember the area map.

"Are there any farms thereabouts?" I ask.

"Of course there weren't any farms. These snowshoes are really dumb animals. They just sat there and I popped them one after the other."

"These aren't snowshoes — they're tame," I say. "Snowshoes don't have pink eyes."

"They must be snowshoes," he insists. We take them home and clean them. Snowshoes!

For the entirety of 1959 I managed three or four hours of pruning, the three boys together about two. There are no mentions of it in 1960, but in 1961 the forester made some remarks about the desirability of pruning — which was not news — and triggered a new wave of efforts.

May 16 — Pruning today. Decide to take a quick walk to the river before beginning. Gigi, the golden

Lab, is ecstatic. She thinks we are going duck hunting, which I do on rare occasions to make her happy and to cater to the family's palate; I don't like to shoot ducks. Of course it's spring now and duck hunting is prohibited. We sit in my duck blind on the river watching the sparkling panorama, the kingfishers diving and then scolding from overhead branches. Gigi wants to go in the water, begs, and I let her. She is standing chest deep, intently watching minnows, when I see a muskrat swimming downstream on a collision course. I want to warn the dog yet not frighten off the muskrat. I wait too long. The muskrat is within two feet of the dog when they see each other. Splash! The muskrat dives; simultaneously the startled dog leaps straight up. For a moment it seems all four of Gigi's feet are out of the water, then she is in my lap. I am partially dry by the time we get back to the hill and I hear the dinner bell. Where has the time gone?

June 20 — This is pruning weekend! We'll really finish up the big trees on the first hill; maybe get a good start on the second hill. There is only one pruning saw, and I have worked out a schedule for each of us. Smith and Paul have paying jobs at a neighbor's farm this afternoon, so they are to prune this morning. Tomorrow we have family obligations, and I book the talent while I can. Meanwhile, I'm tending to plumbing repairs in the pump house. Shouts from the little lake below the first hill. My wife calls me to hurry. Quick!

The canoe has capsized and is floating in the lake. Smith and classmate Roger from the neighboring farm are crawling out of the lake as I arrive. The shore is silty, a mucky ooze that acts like quicksand if one tries to walk out; I have drilled it into the boys to crawl out, if the need arises. Smith and Roger look like coal miners whose showers haven't worked for a week. I'm relieved they are safe.

"What happened?"

Roger says: "I just stopped by when I saw Smith going up the hill, and we got to talking. He said this canoe doesn't tip, and I said every canoe tips."

Our eighteen-foot freighter-type aluminum is flat-bottomed and really hard to tip. I've had it through rapids and white water without mishaps many times.

"And?" I ask.

Confession comes hard to Smith, who tends to leak information out reluctantly, by bits and dribbles — like a miser paying the newspaper boy with pennies, checking each one for condition and rarity.

Smith, it seems, felt compelled to prove the point. They took the canoe out. First Smith stood, rocked it, nothing happened. Then he stood with one foot on each gunwale and rocked. "See, it doesn't tip." He rocked the canoe harder, it still didn't tip.

"See," he said. "It doesn't tip."

"I'll be damned," said Roger, who is not a good swimmer and was nervous. "It really doesn't."

That's when Smith slipped and they capsized.

I swim out, bring the canoe back.

"There's something I'd better tell you," Smith says slowly while I dry off. "Your fishing rod and tackle box were in the canoe. And the tackle box was open."

I send Smith back out in the canoe to fish for the lost gear, using the garden rake, tied to the pruning pole. Fishing pole found at 10:48 A.M. Tackle box and some of contents hooked and ultimately brought on board at 11:53 A.M. Lunch. Rained all afternoon.

Dec. 10 — Snow about two feet deep, wind-packed. Brisk, five above zero. Perfect for working outdoors. Keeping even tempo of work I can shed heavy jacket, work in shirt-sleeves, hat, wool pants, and boots. I try it with and without gloves, and find my hands sufficiently hardened to work without. Pruning goes well; I am half an hour into it when my wife comes out with thermos of hot coffee.

"It's about time I learned to handle snowshoes," she announces, strapping on a pair of bear-paw-type snowshoes. I want to caution her to lift one foot and set it down before raising the other foot, but she is already off the ground in a graceful somersault, and lands headfirst in the snow.

She extricates herself, stands up, and brushes snow from face, ears, and from around her neck. "What did you do to these snowshoes?" she demands.

"Nothing!" I am busily pruning, keeping my back

turned. This is not the time to be caught with even a hint of a smile.

"You could help me," she says.

I lean the saw against a tree, put on my jacket, and buckle on my own snowshoes. We get hers rebuckled, rechecked, and set out slowly on a teaching expedition. It doesn't go too well, but there are no mishaps. I can't explain why it comes easily to me, so hard to her. Maybe bowlegged people do better at it than those who are knock-kneed.

We head out in the clear, away from brush and trees. The snow is deeper here; there are fewer snags and obstacles. I encourage her to speed up a little so as to let the momentum and rhythm help her, and I keep up a running commentary of advice, admonition, and moral support. I'm too busy talking to see the dog, who has a bad habit of following me in the woods and resting on the back of my skis or snowshoes when she tires from walking in the deep snow. The dog is chest deep in snow, decides it is time for a rest, and makes a wild lunge for the back of my wife's snowshoes in hopes of a resting place. Another somersault — my wife's head firmly in the snow — the dog sitting triumphantly on the now-unoccupied snowshoes.

I pick up the pruning saw on the way back to the house.

Entries for 1962: none.

Entries for 1963:

Jan. 17 — It's a Friday and I have given notice that this weekend, regardless of how cold it is, we will prune trees under my supervision; the boys are not to make plans otherwise. It *is* cold — sub-zero at midday for days on end now, no break in weather pattern to be expected. The Winnipeg radio station has excellent weather forecasting that usually applies to us accurately within five degrees. I have become familiar with Canadian place names as a result of listening to the Winnipeg station regularly: Flin Flon, The Pas, Thompson, Reindeer Lake.

As I am backing my car out of the garage to get

to my schoolteaching job, the wheels slip off the worn ruts into softer snow and bury themselves to the axle. I am late, but I disdain the idea of changing clothes and getting heavier boots, so I don't bother. I start digging. Later and later. More digging. Finally get the car moving, in the clear after a few false starts.

Teaching all morning, I feel increasingly hot and uncomfortable. No one else thinks the building is overheated, but I know that it is. My earlobes begin to burn; also the tip of my generously endowed nose. By the time several fingertips burn I know what is coming, and also know there is no help for it. In the lounge I remove shoes and socks. By then the toes, heels, and portions of my soles are burning. They are splotchy white, with a few patches turning pink: I have a moderately severe case of frostbite. Most uncomfortable, but I finish out the day's teaching.

Jan. 18 — Housebound. My family is solicitous, and feels the strong urge to entertain me, which I cannot refuse. Whist.

Jan. 19 — Recuperating from frostbite, I played whist. Also I made up a treasure hunt for the boys. Each has a separate set of clues to be pursued through reference books on our shelves, including the encyclopedia. The trail ultimately leads to a cache of cookies. The clues are hard and require deductive reasoning, not merely looking things up. Derek finally finds *syzygy* in relationship to *apogee* and the most recent space exploit. This in turn confronts him with a clue requiring description of the significance of the compulsory shaving of beards ordered by a Russian ruler of the Middle Ages. Several more, each clue leading to the next, will ultimately direct him to a cache of cookies behind the tub of wild rice. Smith and Paul are off on their separate tracks; when there is time, I tailor-make sets of clues for each of the three boys. I notice Paul using the encyclopedia index with astuteness; good. The boys pester me to lay out these treasure hunts. In summer, when most birthdays fall, a variation on it is a favorite game for outdoor nighttime hunts across fields, through woods; and their friends enjoy it as much as they.

I have a nagging feeling something important is not getting done, but can't place it. Very cold outside; warm and cozy in here. Frostbite is better.

March 10 — Forester Peter Woodiwiss is over in the evening, going over our planting program. The state nursery expects a huge surplus of seedlings. We are asked to accelerate planting — can we handle 65,000 instead of 25,000? I think it's too much; Peter says we should try. We'll have to hire help, make an all-out effort.

"I see you haven't done the pruning yet," he remarks.

"We're working on it, off and on," I tell him.

June 3 — Planned to prune trees on first hill today but Max called saying we could pick up a young pig tomorrow. It's a runt of the current litter and we can have it at less than regular price. I have to fence a pen; I'll fix a stall in the barn.

June 4 — Picked up pig. In five minutes it had located every one of a hundred ways to get out of the pen and had disappeared in the plantation. Looked through the east plantation. No luck.

June 5 — Looked for pig. No luck.

June 6 — Looked for pig. No luck. Gave up at noon. I'm taking a shower preparatory to going to town to shop when Derek yells: "The pig's back! He's in the pen!"

I leap into barn boots and run into the yard. Sure enough, he's in the pen, hungrily feeding at the trough. I'm determined to catch it, put it in the barn. He's keeping one baleful eye on me; one ear is up, the other down, like ambivalent railroad semaphores. But that one eye never leaves me, just as his snout never leaves the trough. I approach steadily, arms outstretched and fingers crooked into talons. Can't wait to get my hands on him, confine him to the barn. By now it's become more important than the few dollars we had to pay for him: it is a one-on-one confrontation. The gap narrows to five feet, four, three —

and I lunge as he steps aside. Again: closer, yet closer, then a dainty step-aside as I grasp.

This time I'll outsmart him: but my faultless flying tackle leaves me full length in the mud as the pig greedily eats from the trough.

Sound of laughter diverts my anger. There are three heads side-by-side in the upstairs window. And my wife is standing by the corner of the house, holding my bath towel. She says: "Thought you might need it if anyone drove in the yard. You forgot to put your clothes on."

Derek yells down: "You need another shower!"

No sympathy and no help. I'll show them.

June 7 — I locked the pig in the barn this morning. I had moved the trough inside last night, leaving the door open. There he was, sound asleep, his belly full and a beatific smile on his face. Not as beatific as mine.

I check the pruning entries for the other years, but they fall into the same dismal pattern. The most recent is from a day last summer, when once again I set out with resolution and the pruning saw, aiming myself at the same 200 trees; screams of extreme anguish and shouts from Peggy brought me racing back. I arrived in time to see Peggy flailing at some highly incensed yellow-jackets with a towel, trying to propel the hysterical Tony and David into the house at the same time. The boys, still under attack from those insects that were evading Peggy, were in pain from the wasp stings and were trying to get their clothes off at the same time that they were attempting to get in the door. Not to be left out of it, I joined the bellowing while I took Tony under one arm, David under the other, and carried them inside. When it was finally quiet, Tony said: "We found the nest in the ground, so we stood on it. Then they can't come out and sting us." The nest had a second exit. And a third.

I conclude that the job of analysis is too much for me at the moment, and had best be laid over for another day. Besides, Smith and Paul are here for the holidays, and I can recruit them for a game of whist.

"Say, Dad," says Smith, shuffling the cards. "You really ought to do something about pruning the trees."

"That's right." I have an idea. "Why don't we go out tomorrow morning. It'll be nice and crisp. Good weather for it."

"Okay," says Smith, more cooperative as an adult than he was as a teenager. "The east plantation looks good; some of the trees are over twenty feet high, and they really need it."

"The east plantation? The new trees?" I can't believe what I'm hearing. "I was thinking of the two hundred old Norways on the first and second hills!"

"Oh, didn't you ever do those?" Smith is dealing now.

"Not all of them, I guess." I've always thought of pruning in terms of the big old trees. It is the only context in which pruning has ever been discussed, planned, put off from day to day and year to year. Yet here is a brand-new dimension, a whole new idea. And it is staggering, because we have planted over 150,000 trees. And Smith is right: some of them are big enough to warrant pruning, and more will reach such a point each year. We could be pruning trees day and night for the next several years!

"Come to think of it," I say, "it might not be a bad day for cross-country skiing and an outdoor picnic tomorrow."

I think that's what we'll be doing, because they all agree so heartily.

13

<hr>

Harvest

I FEEL NOSTALGIC; a touch of midwinter cabin fever? Fragments of bygone images float into my consciousness: Smith, Paul, and Derek and their friends leaping out of the second-story window of the barn into a snowdrift, sliding to the ground, whooping, occasionally buried in the deep snow and digging out amid laughter. Derek trying to scare a greedy blue jay off the bird feeder so that the evening grosbeaks might return to it, and succeeding only in breaking the windowpane. Snowbound and without electricity, bundled in sleeping bags on the living room floor and playing Scrabble, whist, bridge.

I distinguish between recollection of past experience and nostalgia. The purpose of recollection is to learn, to profit, to put something that is here-and-now into perspective aided by an earlier event. Nostalgia on the other hand can be a means of escaping from present problems by latching onto earlier pleasures. What triggers my nostalgia? That I cannot think of the cause suggests it is so vexing that I have shoved it to the back of my mind. A quick inventory of personal and family relationships provides no clues; nor do my work, business, and tree farm concerns yield an answer.

The date? Some special event memorialized in my subconscious? Yes. On this day many years ago, when I was eight years old, much of my external world collapsed and my family life and relationships were changed as well. It was the day that armed fascists overthrew the government in Austria and in a bloody few days of street fighting destroyed democratic institutions and the existence I had, until then, known. Gone were the easy associations with peers, the playground and the youth center; gone was my father's role in public life, his relationships and importance and his social effectiveness. My adult radicalism stemmed largely from these events, reinforced by the ultimate losses suffered four years later when the Nazis invaded and gave the coup de grace to my mortally wounded childhood.

From then on I fought for what I perceived to be libertarian values, and opposed the arch-fiend: oppression of human rights. I organized, wrote, participated in organizations; I picketed, worked, exhorted, demonstrated; a few times I was arrested. ("Daddy, the kids said you were in jail. Were you? Why?")

Good efforts — worth the fight, most of them. But insufficient in that they did not provide me with my basic personal needs: a social and intellectual setting where I had a feeling of belonging and acceptance; a sense of being a constructive person as well as a sense of doing constructive things; an aesthetic environment that would please my love of the outdoors; a life of greater symmetry and balance.

These were needs that influenced the birth of the tree farm, of this way of life.

Then why the nostalgia tonight? Birth of tree farm . . . death . . . of course! It's the harvest. The *cutting* of the trees.

Cutting trees that one has planted is a little like death: an irrevocable action. I've taken my own Christmas trees from the natural woods and from the wild, unwilling to cut one we'd planted ourselves. But necessity and prudent ecological management have brought harvest close. Cutting the trees is a form of death, but it is also a form of death to let the trees grow. Yesteryear's seedlings are now twenty-five to thirty feet high, a foot thick at the butt; and some are much too close to each other. Soon they will crowd each other to the point of mutual damage and exhaustion — two stags with horns locked in competition and unable to free themselves.

They grew so slowly the first few years — a few inches a year at the most. Then they set roots more deeply, grew faster, a foot a year, then two, and sometimes three. Now the time of harvest is coming like first-morning tints; first wisps of breeze after wind-still night are brushing my cheek.

I'd given Derek 300 trees for a Christmas present. "If you cut and haul them, you should be able to sell them in the Cities and make out quite nicely. Do you want them?"

"Oh, yes. That's great! Of course I have exams at the university and don't have much time. But I think we can manage. Yes!"

"Take them from the east plantation, from the far northeast corner. Every other tree; they're too thick there."

"Okay."

"I won't be around; I've got to be away . . ."

"We'll manage. Thanks."

I wanted to caution Derek that the enterprise would work only if he did the cutting and hauling himself, that otherwise the profit margin would be very small. But the telephone connection was broken, and I solaced myself that we had talked about the economics of the tree business often enough that he would know this.

Work obligations kept me away, and it was after Christmas that Derek, looking haggard and unhappy, told me about it. His examination schedule had been more demanding than he had anticipated, and on his only trip to the farm he had enlisted the help of erstwhile high school friends who lived and worked nearby. They had agreed to do the cutting and hauling for a fee; meanwhile, Derek and his wife, Elissa, would secure a lot in Minneapolis. The trees would arrive about the time the exams ended, and he could be at the lot to sell them. But the plan went awry.

"Where are the trees?" Derek pleaded with his friend over the phone. First the truck wasn't working, then the saw broke down. The help didn't show and his friend had domestic problems.

Derek — tied by exams, his frustrations fed by the passing days and his inability to do anything about the delay — became more vociferous in his demands; his friend became more dilatory. Finally the old friendship ruptured, and friends of friends were found to do the work — and had to be paid.

"I couldn't believe it when the truck pulled up," Derek later told me. "The trees were so huge, so bushy, they couldn't possibly fit into anybody's living room."

I had been recalcitrant about "shaping" the trees over the years — a pruning process whereby new growth is cut off with a machete to remove extra-long branches and to give the Norway pines a more traditional Christmas tree shape. So although I knew these trees would have their natural, uneven shapes, I did not expect them to be too large and too bushy; neither did Derek.

He and Elissa did what cutting and trimming they could on their loaned neighborhood-center lot, obtained lights, made signs, and distributed handbills. They opened for business, but few people came. The neighborhood residents were too poor; there was not enough passerby traffic composed of more affluent buyers.

"People came at night and ripped us off," Derek said. "I took my sleeping bag to the lot and slept there. That stopped most of it."

Then they decided to flock the trees, to spray them in garish pink, blue, white, to each customer's order. A few more trees were sold. When it was over — after several sleepless nights, the end of a long and close friendship, and much distress — he had lost money.

"A nightmare," he said, and Elissa concurred. "Never again."

I did not have the heart to tell him that the trees had been cut from the sparser west plantation, not the overcrowded east planting. No wonder they were too large, too bushy: these west-plantation trees had been properly spaced and distanced already, and were on their way to becoming posts and poles. The crowded ones were more suitable in size, had a better shape, and now still needed thinning. I smart at the sight of the open gaps in the west, and feel anew dismay at the waste. Most of all I regret that my well-intentioned gift was ill-timed and that it misfired, bringing grief and a broken friendship for my son.

But it's not concern with the past that triggered nostalgia the other night, it is that I must face up to harvest preparations of my own. It's an adjustment that I have to make, and that everyone in the family will have to prepare for. The east planting has to be gone over; trees have to be selected for posts, others marked for poles. Many should be trimmed and sheared ac-

236 THE TREE FARM

cordingly, because in a year or two the first ones must come out. They are growing too close in spots. Here and there on the west side we will have to do the same. Timing of the harvest is still indeterminate: one, two, three years from now. Maybe four. But the preparatory work and planning must start now.

I fret about how the older boys will feel about it, but I think I'm really coping with my own feelings. Tree farming has a particular effect on my sense of time — on how I perceive its passage. I measure it in days and hours like everyone else, and in the seasons of the year, as do farmers and gardeners and others aware of their external surroundings. But growing trees makes me perceive of time in decades and longer spans as well. I look forward and backward in terms of generations, and this gives me an added sense of personal place in the scheme of things. We each assert our thrust, our will to live, in different ways. This happens to be mine. Not my only way of course; being able to give and receive love is another. So is creativity and constructiveness in many forms.

Coming to grips with the harvest makes me philosophical.

It just is not feasible for everyone to come to the farm at the same time; I'd hoped for a big family gathering this summer, taking advantage of school vacations. But Paul's school schedule and the demands of the genetic research laboratory he has established tie him down for now. He will bring Mary and their new baby, Ramona, later in the summer. Derek and Elissa are kept away by their work as well — Derek developing a new documentary movie script, Elissa on a new job directing a halfway house for schizophrenics.

Smith is camping on the back hill with my grandchildren Robbie and Annette. I'm invited over for marshmallows, which I don't crave all that much, and for companionship, on which I thrive.

"We saw a beaver," Robbie announces. "He slapped his tail."

"Two beavers," Annette corrects him. She is very much the older sister, ladylike. Both are straight-backed, vigorous youngsters with a wide variety of ever-changing interests. It is difficult to believe Annette is entering junior high school soon.

"The game wardens helped us restock the lake," I tell them. "The beavers were damming up a creek that flooded out a road east of Pennington. The game wardens trapped them in boxes and brought them here last fall in time to stock winter food."

Tony and David have their mouths stuffed with marshmallows, but manage to convey that they, too, had seen the beavers. Then all four scamper off to climb trees, and we see them shortly after, each perched near the top of a plantation Norway, shouting to each other. They are too far away for Smith and me to make out the game they are playing, but it has a good burble to it. Smith and I sit on the ground near the little campfire and savor the woodsmoke; the pine scent; the vista of older trees, plantation, and, in the near distance, the lake.

"The kids and I walked through the east plantation

this morning," Smith says, poking an empty marsh-mallow stick at the fire, playing with the embers. "The trees are pretty crowded. Especially in the second- and third-year plantings."

I know the ones he means. We put them in in 1960, 1961, and 1962, before the huge planting in 1963 that was wiped out by the drought.

Smith goes on: "I think you're going to have to thin them out. Maybe mark the ones most likely for posts and poles in a few years, and start shearing them so you can see what you're doing."

I don't say anything because I'm surprised. This is what I had wanted to tell him, but had not known how to begin. I think Smith misunderstands my silence, and thinks I'm feeling bad about having to cut the trees. He goes on.

"I'd be glad to come and help as I can."

"I'd like that," I tell him. "I know it's got to be done, and had planned to get started with the marking and shearing this fall."

"It wouldn't be a bad idea to put in some more fire-breaks while you're at it," he encourages me. "Maybe when I come back from exhibiting at the Renaissance Fair in September."

He has been invited to exhibit his art and craft work again this year, an acknowledgment of the quality and artistry he has achieved over the years.

"Fall would be a good time," I agree. "Now tell me what you'll be showing at the fair this year." And we talk about his recent efforts with redwood burl and with inlays.

I'm glad for the private talk and touched that he anticipated the need to harvest and my feelings.

A peculiar weather pattern for midsummer: hot and dry in daytime, positively chilly at night (and the wood-burning range is in service). Paul, Mary, and Ramona are here for a few days. It is too chilly for comfortable camping so they are sleeping in the house. The dogs are banished — either leashed or sleeping in the car — because Mary has declared emphatically that the drive back to Duluth with a recently skunk-sprayed dog is a problem that should be avoided at all costs.

Paul is talking about the genetics research, and his participation in an international congress concluded the week before. "The technology of the lab is good enough that we can work on genetic transmission of susceptibility to certain diseases." It is an esoteric and new field of exploration, and I cannot follow all of the scientific nuances and implications of the processes he describes, but I am impressed by the thrust and the intent of the research, which I do grasp. I am also intrigued that Paul wants to become a general practitioner in a rural community, yet is also deeply involved in this pioneering laboratory work. The interest in biologic research is a by-product of his premedical courses, and, somehow, of his undergraduate work in philosophy.

Mary will resume her undergraduate work in biology this fall, and there's much animated talk in the living room. In a corner Ramona stirs, croons in her sleep. She has Mary's red hair.

"I forgot to warn you," I say, having just remembered. "Be extra careful with garbage this year. We lime it right away each time it goes on the compost pile. It's been a bad year for berries and we've got bears around."

I'd known we had a bear living near the river for at least two years, and I didn't want to bring it closer by tempting it with garbage smells.

"When we first came here it just wouldn't have seemed possible to have bears living here," Paul mused.

"Or wildcats," I add. "And now we can hear them screech at night sometimes."

Surprise! Derek and Elissa are here, after a tiring bus ride, lugging a big box in addition to their packs and luggage. They had said some time before they would try to come, but not having heard further we all concluded it would not be possible for them. Now they are here.

After supper Derek orders us around like a sergeant major, arranging chairs and setting up equipment. It reminds me that I was more authoritarian, peremptory with the older boys. Peggy has taught me a great deal about becoming a better parent, and I think I am warmer, more loving and responsive, with Tony and David than I was with Smith, Paul, and Derek. (But then, we all like to think kindly of ourselves.)

"Lights out!" Derek orders.

I have been hearing about Derek's film for a year now, and Elissa has had to live with the frenetic pro-

duction and strips of film in their tiny apartment
nearly as long. I know what it is about: life as perceived by a severely afflicted cerebral-palsy victim
who has been institutionalized all the twenty-some
years of his life. Derek has worked with this young
man for months, communicating through a letter
board on which his friend jerkily pointed to letters to
make up the words. In this painfully slow way ideas
were exchanged; the script was written, and eventually the film was shot and edited. The first critical re-
view, in a Minneapolis daily newspaper, praised the
film strongly as being exciting and profound — project-
ing the viewer into the world of the cerebral-palsied
person.

As the film flickers on the sheet hung on the living
room wall, and as the rented projector whirrs, I find
myself unprepared for what I see. Though I have been
hearing about the birth pains of this movie, I am
caught — trapped by its emotional impact, its pictorial and human force. *I* am existing unable to speak
or to move without assistance; *I* am at the mercy of
attendants and custodial workers for every physical
need; *I* am victim to the whim of the cab driver who
leaves me — strapped in my wheelchair and covered
by a cloud of exhaust — unwilling to be bothered with
a cripple; *I* am living out an existence devoid of sex, of
love, of friendship and human contact, much as I crave
all these.

My son makes me see and experience this through
the film he has created and is showing me; I am moved
and must wipe tears as we turn on the lights when it is

over, and we sit in silence for a while. As my feelings subside I realize the production is technically and artistically very good.

Paul and Derek help me carry fence posts and signs across the edge of the east plantation to the corner. It is the place where they had helped plant spruce in the half-mile-long strip, fifty feet wide, the year before. We need to put up a warning for wintertime snow-mobilers so that the seedlings won't be damaged. Tony and David are trailing along, poking at gopher mounds and alternately racing ahead and staying close, in the way of young children. They are still at an age when the needs for independence and dependence fluctuate unpredictably in a relatively short span of time.

The chore is done quickly and we agree to walk back through the plantation, ducking around trees. It is magnificent for playing hide and seek. We gather, out of breath, in a little open spot.

"I've counted seven deer beds so far," Paul pants. The plantation has become a haven for wildlife and for birds.

"And I've counted nineteen furrows, each one a foot deep," counters Derek, who tends to focus on wildlife and the outdoors from a pictorial vantage rather than from a participatory one.

We can hear Tony and David, but they are hiding again, demanding to be found.

"Smith says he's going to help you get it ready for harvest," Paul says. "Maybe I can come over and lend a hand."

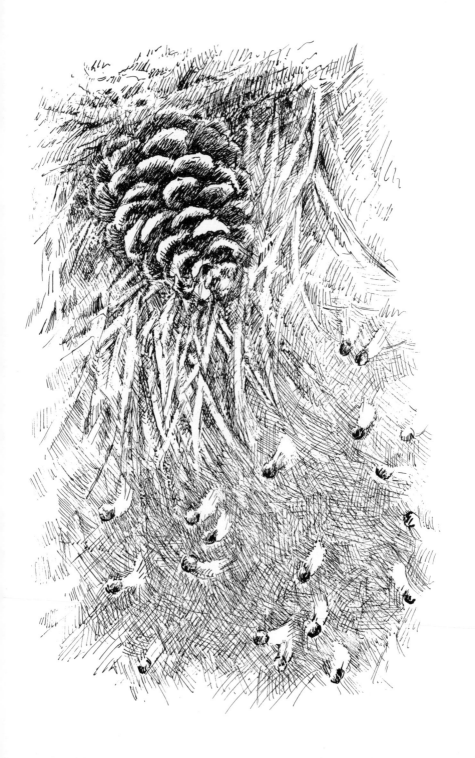